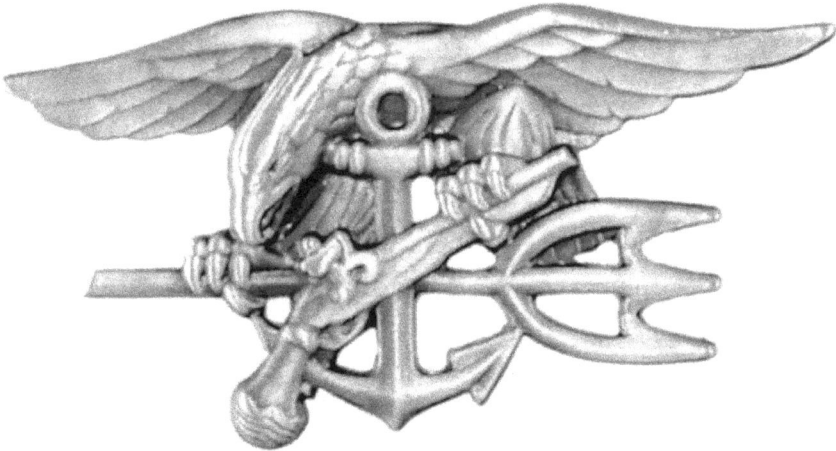

SHAKE ME IF IT'S SUNNY

DEEP SEA DIVING TALES
BY
BILLY RAY LEDFORD

For information regarding permission, please write to:
info@barringerpublishing.com
Barringer Publishing, Naples, Florida
www.barringerpublishing.com

Cover, graphics, layout design by Linda S. Duider

ISBN: 978-1-954396-32-6
Library of Congress Cataloging-in-Publication Data
Shake Me If It's Sunny / Ledford

Printed in U.S.A.

TABLE OF CONTENTS

PREFACE

This book is written about the offshore diving industry. Set in the early 1980s, it is primarily about commercial divers but I haven't left out the Navy, Sport Divers, and the odd ball things they get up to on the job and off. They are hard working but even harder players. They take danger in their stride daily. They live with the constant threat of violent death. So maybe they have the right to live the way they do—drinking, partying, chasing women, and in general just raising hell.

Let it be known that all names, places, and dates in this book are totally fictitious; this was done to protect the guilty. Because we know that all divers are guilty of something.

Also, let it be known that if you are a diver, you will probably think you recognize yourself or some of your diving buddies. You are most likely correct.

Some of the stories in this book are completely true, some are embellished, some are exaggerated, and some of them are downright lies; you will have to figure which are which for yourselves.

If you are a mild-mannered, gentle person and your sensitivity is easily offended, STOP NOW. Do not read this book.

This book is rude, crude, nasty, critical, inconsiderate, and, in some cases, filthy. If you are thin skinned, you will bleed to death. Like the Chinese say:

"YOU WILL DIE A DEATH OF A THOUSAND CUTS"

ACKNOWLEDGEMENTS

Writing a book is harder than I thought and more rewarding than I could have ever imagined. None of this would have been possible without my wife and best friends.

I would like to say a special thank you to the following people:

My wife, Karen, without her support and help in the early days, none of this would have been possible.

My son and agent, Warren. Without him pushing me, this book would have probably passed into oblivion, never to have seen the light of day.

As life marches on, people come and go, friends also. Below, I would like to say thank you to you all, as at some point you were my best friends, shaping my adventures and in some way this book.

Fred Wallard: Was always a hard, true, loyal friend. Sadly, Fred has passed and will never see this but will never be forgotten. Fred was inducted to the Divers Hall of Fame.

Denny Schwartz: Was my right-hand man, always my go to guy. Denny was also inducted to the Divers Hall of Fame.

Arnie Finch: Was always the third wheel but was always a welcomed third wheel. Another who will never see this—enjoy the great ride in the sky.

Chuck Gains: Hell of a diver. Always liked to party just as hard as he dove. Always kept me laughing and smiling.

Bernie Swarchertfeger: Was my best wingman, unfortunately Bernie and I lost contact many years ago. Another that will never see this.

Last, I would like to thank Barringer Publishing and the editing team. I know this was not an easy book to work on.

INTRODUCTION

Recently, there has been a period in my life where I have had very little to do. This was something that I was completely unprepared for, as I have spent what seems like all my life being involved in some form or fashion in the diving industry.

So, being at loose ends, I decided to do what every diver at some time has said that he is going to do, and that is to write down some of the tales that are so prevalent in the diving game; the original intention was to merely occupy my time but as I've progressed, it began to look as if I might actually get a short book out of all those sea stories that divers have been telling and experiencing for a great many years. So, finally I said to myself, *Why the hell not; go for it.*

Let me start this introduction by saying that I am not an author, and undoubtedly never will be. As a matter of fact, my wife says that the only thing I am any good at writing is my signature when I sign the pay checks so she can deposit them in her bank account. But the reason I have attempted to write this collection of sea stories, and fairy tales, is that it didn't seem right that they should just pass into oblivion without being recorded. These things that happened in the last twenty years of my diving career will not mean a thing to 95% of the people that read them, but the 5% that are left will certainly understand and I hope even to appreciate that they have been placed in print. That is if I can find some publisher daft enough to want to print a pile of rubbish.

The diving industry is rapidly changing. As with most industries of today, it is entering the age of the computer (I wouldn't have attempted to write this book if it wasn't for my little, home micro with a word processing program. It gives even a dumb-ass diver the heaven-sent chance to write "almost" legibly). The times that a large portion of these stories occur are gone; gone are the days of 350 foot surface orientated gas dives; gone are the days of 600 feet plus bounce dives; gone are the days of using scuba gear in the commercial diving game; gone is the macho diver. Nowadays, a diver is part of a team and there is no room for the individuality that used to exist in the industry. I am not saying that there are no characters left, it's just that they are not allowed to perform like they could in the past. I am not saying this is bad. For, in most cases, it's much better—the diving safety has improved many times over.

We used to say that in the diving game there would always be a need for divers. Now, I have really started to doubt that is true. We see everyday the sophisticated, unmanned vehicles doing jobs that only a few short years ago required a diver; almost all the inspection jobs are being done by ROVs. Cleaning of platforms, ships etc., are done 90% of the time by ROVs, and the wiz kids are still hard at work, engineering, designing, developing new tools, vehicles, and vessels to replace the diver. And let's not overlook the fact that for all practical purposes, the commercial diver is working at what many knowledgeable persons in the industry consider his depth limitation at the present time—that is to say around 1000 feet. There has been some research for practical dives to 1500 feet but there has not really been any commercial dives to these depths that have been successfully accomplished.

The oil companies, having set their sights on very deep water, and by very deep I mean depths well over 1500 feet, at present are drilling exploration wells in depths exceeding 5000 feet. I don't know what feelings or thoughts that the majority of the professional divers have regarding diving to these tremendous depths, but I do know this old diver will not be spending any bottom time down there. My point being, if the oil companies are looking for oil in those depths of water, they are thinking about exploiting it at some time in the not too distant future, and I personally don't believe that the diving industry will be able to put divers into those kinds of depths at ambient pressures. If man goes at all, it will almost certainly be in a pressure resistance suit which is really nothing more than a one-man mini sub. And, in the larger submersibles that are presently being developed, it sure as hell doesn't require a diver to fly one of those beasts.

But this book is not about the gloomy time ahead, it is about the good old days of the past when there were good times had by all. My original intention when I started this book was to write just about the humorous things that happened. I have only been partially successful; I found that I couldn't stay completely away from some of the more serious subjects in the diving field but I don't think they will distract too drastically from the pleasure that I hope it will bring some of you old divers. And who knows, maybe even the young divers might find something they can understand and appreciate.

SO, STAND BY BECAUSE HERE WE GO!!

CHAPTER
ONE

Becoming A Diver

How does a man go about becoming that 'WEIRD CREATURE,' the Deep Sea Diver—The Demon of the Deep, the Aquanaut, the Frogman, the Air Diver, the Saturation Diver—even the lowest of the low, the Scuba Diver (more commonly known as a 'Scubby Dooby'). Not a term of endearment. But Scubby Dooby is usually associated with a sports diver, or 'a weekend disaster area', or someone known to a professional who would be better off if you gave him a loaded gun and told him to go play on the motorway blindfolded, or someone who would be referred to while sinking a few pints down at the local as someone who doesn't know his "ASS FROM A HOLE IN THE GROUND."

So, how do you become a Commercial Diver? First and most important, you must be intelligent, smart, knowledgeable, strong, handsome (good looking won't do), conceited, egotistic, and have an unlimited capacity for strong beverages. Other important factors to be considered are bravery, foolhardiness and a 'don't give a damn' attitude. An accomplished bullshitter is an absolute must, and it also helps if you are proficient at eating razor blades and glass (razor blades being of a secondary importance, if you haven't impressed '. . . the bird by the time you need to shave,' you are in the shit anyway). Besides, you can't impress as many people while shaving as you can in a bar eating wine glasses, or even pint mugs if you are a macho man. But probably, the single most important characteristic trait is the ability to be a superb actor. The characteristics are: cleverness, slyness, and deviousness, but you must never outwardly show any of these. You will see many examples of these traits as we progress through the adventures of the fearless fighting frogmen.

So, assuming the prospective diver candidate has most of these attributes, how does he set about becoming a DEEP SEA DIVER EXTRAORDINAIRE?

That can be summed up with one three letter word—LIE. One example that comes to mind happened to a new operations manager about ten years ago in Scotland. This man had only recently been promoted. He had been working offshore for years as a diving superintendent. He knew just about everything about commercial diving that could be known. He knew all the sly, dirty tricks that divers could get up to. He knew how to handle them when they were stumbling, staggering, falling down drunk, or when their umbilical was fouled on the bottom in 300 feet of water with nothing on the gauge but "USE NO OIL", so it would be safe to assume he would know a real diver when he interviewed Joe for a job as a 'Sat Diver.' (For you dummies, sat is short for saturation a term used for a diver who has been down long enough for his body tissues to have become saturated with inert gases). So, to make a long story short, our budding ops manager hired Joe after about an hour of a bullshit/name dropping session in which he was positive that he had finally found the diver of his dreams—a man that could walk, talk, and chew gum, all at the same time. He had Joe fill out a job application, sent him for a diving medical and then sat back, picked up Joe's job application and with great satisfaction looked over Joe's extensive list of diving accomplishments, i.e., 700 plus air dives to 200 feet, 450 surface orientated gas dives to 300 feet, over 300 days in saturations, all construction dives down to 650 feet.

Our man sent Joe out the very next day to a job where he needed a good man. He patted himself on the back considering what a fine job he was doing for his company.

He couldn't see the problems his predecessor had had, that had driven him to such extremes of drink.

He was now down south somewhere drying out, "Oh well, he always was a weak cunt."

Needless to say, that was not the end of the story.

Two days later, he received a radio call from his old mate, the offshore diving superintendent, whom he had personally trained and of whom he was very proud. They had dived and partied halfway around the world together; if there was a man that he would trust, here was that man.

He suspected that there might be a problem when the diving superintendent didn't even say good morning, let alone, "how the hell is your hammer hanging." What issued out of the radio speaker was not exactly what you could classify as proper radio procedures. What did blare out was, "Where in the hell did you get this asshole that you sent out here? He doesn't know his ass from a hole in the ground. He's so stupid he doesn't know the difference between a come-a-long and a donkey dick, not to mention, how to rig a come-a-long to pull a donkey's dick." As you are undoubtedly aware by the above quote, this sort of set our man back onto his heels but being the promising young man on the team, noted for his quick thinking, he replied, "Give Joe a couple of days; he is suffering from jet lag; I know this guy is alright because I checked him out myself." The superintendent agreed to give Good 'Ol Joe another chance, but said he wasn't too damn happy about doing so.

That very afternoon our fearless hero was checking some job application files that were a few months old to see what gems he could glean from the bunch of wankers, when he discovered another job application from Good 'Ol Joe. *Hum, only six months old*, and then, as he read this second job application, (which, in reality, was the first job application), the horrible truth dawned. Good 'Ol Joe had lied to him. There it was in black and white, in Joe's very own handwriting, "I have just recently graduated from Blankety Blank Diving School and I'm seeking employment with a reputable firm such as yours. Please find attached a copy of my resumé for your information etc. etc. and laid out neatly on the form where it asked for diving experience it read:

Air dives	30
Maximum depth	40
Surface gas	none
Max depth	N/A
Bell dives	none
Maximum depth	N/A
Saturation days	none
Maximum depth	N/A

Well, Good 'Ol Joe managed to get out of the country without our irate hero getting his hands on him (and thank God for that).

Now, I can tell you think I misled you regarding lying to get ahead in the diving industry. Well, let me reassure you, I have told nothing but the truth, because you see, Good 'Ol Joe is working (I won't say where) as operations manager for, in his own words, "a reputable diving company."

You aren't going to believe this, but our hero still carries both copies of those job applications, waiting for his 'golden moment of sweet revenge.' He now lives by the motto, DON'T GET MAD, DON'T GET EVEN, GET AHEAD. If Good 'Ol Joe reads this, let him be warned.

The "Fearless" Diver

Another incident that could be considered typical of the diving game, regarding that all important first job and lying your way into it, actually happened on a job that I was in charge of. I was working offshore for one of the world's largest construction companies, working on a project for one of the major oil companies. This particular project was very dive orientated and required a large team of divers for the work that needed to be done. In this situation, it was the installation of cathodic protection anodes that were being post-installed due to a design error in the original construction of the jacket. When an oil company is spending close on a hundred thousand dollars a day for equipment and crews to do a job, they rightly expect personnel to be qualified and sufficiently experienced to perform their assigned tasks.

There was no humor in this story at the time, but now it brings a chuckle to me every time that I think of it. We were diving twenty-four hours a day, seven days a week and even with a large crew we were short of divers, so I sent a call to the beach with a request for some more of them 'FEARLESS DEEP SEA DIVERS,' only to be told that there was a shortage of divers at the time. (Oh, for the good old days) but they would see what they could round up. Sounds like a ROUND-UP. Oh well, most people think of divers as just so many dumb animals anyway.

The next day on the supply boat, they arrived—four, young, gung-ho, wet behind the ears, so-called divers.

They were given one day to work with the crew before we put them into the water; this gave them a chance to become familiarized with the job we were doing and a chance for us to see what their capabilities were. Well, after the first day, it was down to the nut cutting. Our experienced divers were all burned out; the moment of truth had finally arrived. To be fair, I thought the three youngest divers didn't have a hope in hell of going into the water and doing anything but blowing bubbles. The eldest (if I remember right was twenty-two years old) I felt could just maybe accomplish something, so I held him back as stand-by diver just in case one of the youngsters should get into trouble and require assistance (like I mean, SAVE HIM FROM DROWNING). Much to my surprise, the three young'uns did dive, did get a little work done, didn't drown, an accomplishment in itself, and did arrive back on the surface in one piece. (Really still even had all their fingers). Ah, I can hear you say, time for my hero to dive, and you would be right. When we informed him, it was his dive and to get ready, he said, "I'm not going down there, it's too goddamn dangerous!" After we had recovered our composure, we asked him the question that was uppermost in our minds: "would he please expand on his statement." To which he replied, "I'm not a diver, I was just having a drink in a pub the other night and talking to a guy who asked me if I was a diver. I told him hell yes, one of the best! That impressed him so much that I couldn't turn him down when he offered me a diving job. So here I am, besides, I've never been offshore before, and I wanted to see what it was all about. Anyway, I thought I could dive; it doesn't look all that hard on television."

As you might imagine, the diving crew was not overly impressed but at least it gave us something to giggle about, and I won't bring up the ammunition it provided the crew to use against the gentleman who did his hiring in the local pub. Can you see it in your mind's eye? The look of egg spread over his face, and I will never forget what his bar bill was the night the crew arrived from offshore, (I must stop there, because those are different stories that I just might get around to telling someday, and you can bet your knickers that they all will be true, well almost true).

By the way, two of those young'uns are still in the diving game and are considered very good divers. Just goes to show you, you can never be sure.

Now that you are getting used to listening to bullshit, here is a real training story.

The California Frogman

George came from a well-to-do family in Northern California, his father was a doctor and his older brother was a lawyer. His father wanted George to finish college, get a good education, and make something out of himself to uphold the family image. George would rather party, drink beer and chase pussy, and these things, enjoyable as they are, are not conductive to good grades in school. Besides George had seen on television an old rerun of the movie, *THE FROGMEN,* so George decided that he wanted to be a frogman—so much more glamorous and rewarding than being a mere doctor or lawyer.

After seventeen weeks of grueling military training, some say the hardest military training in the world. (I hear all you, SAS, SBS, etc. shouting "That's bullshit, our training is ten times more difficult than those candy asses," Oh sorry, candy arses go through). Anyway, after seventeen weeks of hell, mud, blood, shit, sweat, and tears, George graduates from the U.S. Navy's Underwater Demolition school and is a fully-fledged Navy frogman. George, being as proud as a pig in shit, can't wait to call his father and let him share in his joy.

George calls his beloved father and says, "Dad, I've done it, I've graduated from the Navy's Underwater Demolition school, I'm a frogman." After a lengthy pause, his father says, "Your brother is a lawyer, your father is a doctor, and you, (with a tremble and a note of disapproval in his voice) you're a fucking frogman!"

But in all sincerity, most divers nowadays are ex-Navy divers or have attended one of the many recognized diving training schools located throughout the world. These schools are, in most cases, well run and offer a good basic training for their students. Unfortunately, most of these are in business to make money, and in order to keep their training classes full, they promise their students that once they graduate, (after shelling out a mere £10,000 to £15,000, or an equivalent sum, for the fine opportunity of becoming one of those glorious underwater heroes), every major diving company in the world will be beating a path to their doors, bidding against each other just to have the privilege of hiring such competent and highly trained individuals as themselves. And not only that, they're sure that they will pay off that huge pile of money that they borrowed from dear old dad, or their local bank manager in the first couple of weeks after they graduate, because everybody knows that deep sea divers are rich. Why hell, in a year or two, they know they will be rolling in the dough, sporting around town, with a dolly bird on each arm. That Dino they've been admiring down at the local Wop Shop will be theirs, along with that new turbocharged, go-faster, super bike from Chinkyland. They see it all—a pocket full of money and a heart full of desire. Six months holiday every year in Bermuda (everybody knows that divers only work six months a year), nothing but the best Russian Caviar and finest French Champagnes. Oh, it truly is going to be a wonderful life.

Now for the bitter truth, let's start with the only thing they got right. It is absolutely true that divers only work about six months out of the year. That is because there is no work the rest of the year, especially in the North Sea where it is not uncommon to have storms with waves 50 to 60 feet high, and the occasional 100-year storm with waves reaching as much as 100 feet. Even the rough tough North Sea Divers aren't able to dive in weather and seas like that.

And the chances of a major diving company hiring this gung-ho, wet behind the ears, super star, straight out of diving school are almost non-existent . . . (Back to our old saying, he doesn't know his ass from a hole in the ground) . . .

I've had these punk rockers come into my office looking for a job, straight out of Fort Apache Training Centre, with stars in their eyes ready to hit the big time. When they were offered a job offshore as an air diver to give them a chance to find out what the real world is all about and to get a little real diving experience, I've had them turn the offer down saying, "I'm a SATURATION DIVER, not an AIR DIVER." Well, all I can say is, best of luck to them, and their daydreams, or should I have said wet dreams?

Then there is all that money out there just waiting for you to come along and collect it. Like shit. A diver has to be the worst paid professional in the world. For the risks he takes by putting his

ASS on the line every time he makes a dive, he literally receives peanuts. So, forget all that high rolling, champagne, caviar, and other bullshit; you will be eating beans, drinking beer, if you are lucky and scratching with the chickens.

What all this amounts to is at the end of the day, 90+% of these young hopefuls are going to end up just like the almost four million other unemployed workers in Britain. On the dole, married with a house full of screaming rug rats and a bathroom full of shitty diapers (nappies). And I haven't even mentioned that sweet young, slim, trim, 9 stone, lovely beauty that he married. She now weighs 14 stones and is constantly nagging at him to get up off his lazy arse (for you dumbass Yanks, read arse as ass) and go out and get himself a respectable job, such as a rubbish collector.

But, again, at the end of the day, it will not make any difference what I say, because there are just too many dumbasses like me out there that know in their hearts it won't be like that for them. They are special. They shall overcome, instead of scratching with the chickens. They are going to soar with the eagles.

Now, I will tell you the easy way to become a commercial deep sea diver. That is, if you don't want to spend about four years of your life joining the Navy to get all that free training, or if dear old Dad won't lend you 15,000 Quid, or if the bank manager locks the door when he sees you coming, take what money you have and book yourself a holiday to one of the numerous tourist traps anywhere in the world

Author, Billy Ray Ledford

where there is plenty of sand, sun and salt water. Here you will be able to lay on the beach, sip *Pina Coladas*, watch the beach bunnies, and work on your tan. And if you really have your heart set on being a deep sea diver, pay a visit to the local yacht marina, where you will undoubtedly find a gentleman who will be willing to teach and train you, (for only a small percentage of your holiday cash) in all the finer points that are required for you to become a 'Deep Sea Diver Extraordinaire.' He will personally teach you all the Diving Physics, Diving Safety etc. that you will need to know to be a commercial diver. He will even take you to some nice sandy beach, strap a set of scuba tanks on your back and check you out on open ocean diving, so that you will be well and truly trained for your new career. Then he returns you to the marina and you have written him a nice, fat check/cheque (he may insist on cash, so be

Navy flag football championships. Author, Billy Ray Ledford, is in the back row second from the left.

prepared). He will then issue you a very pretty "Official Diving Certificate."

And the beauty of this is it doesn't take up much of your holiday, because you will be able to be back on the beach that afternoon, watching the dolly birds, sipping a tall cool one, working on that tan that every diver has (don't forget that tan is important, no company will hire you if you don't have one) and admiring your pretty, new certificate, proclaiming to one and all that you are a qualified DEEP SEA DIVER EXTRAORDINAIRE.

When you arrive back in the land of ice and snow and have recovered from your hangover and sunburn, you must make a trip to oil city, where all the major diving companies are located. This is where it takes perseverance. You then make an appointment with the operations manager for an interview. Don't be put off by his secretary, be firm and you will get to see him. After all, you are the one who is doing him a favor; he is the one that needs you!

When you do get in to see him be positive, tell him you have come to solve all his diving problems, that you are ready to take on the toughest job he's got (that will impress him to no end) and when he asks you what your background and experience are, just show him your certificate. That's all you need to do; your certificate will speak for itself.

He may look a little surprised when he looks at your certificate, after all he doesn't see too many of them; he may even ask you if the certificate is any good? If he asks you this question, just be honest and tell him, HELL,YES. At this point, the chances are 99 out of a hundred that he is going to smile at you and tell you to, "stick it up your ass, because good things won't hurt you"; then roaring with laughter he is going to boot your ass out of his office.

But don't let this little set back affect your morale. Carry on to the next company, and you will find that it's much easier to get in to see the man in charge. You will most likely find there are a number of people there to greet you. That's because the first operation manager has called all his opposite numbers in the other companies to let them know that you are on your way, and they need a good laugh, too.

The point that I have been trying to make is that if you want to be a commercial diver, it behooves you to do it right. Try faking it, and the very least is you are going to get caught. If you don't get caught by the people with whom you are working then the sea will catch you sooner or later and kill you dead as a door nail. But the real tragic event would be if you killed someone else with your stupidity. And that is a very real possibility.

If, at the end of the day, you don't want to be a Commercial Diver but would like to do some Sports Diving, for the sake of your own life, don't go to some 'COWBOY OUTFIT' that puts you in the water in a few hours. You are going to get hurt; go to a recognized training school that takes its time and properly teaches you the right way. You will live a hell of a lot longer. Never underestimate the seas, they will kill the foolish and inexperienced before you can bat your eye.

I will personally recommend to any person that has ever entertained the idea of taking up scuba diving as a hobby, to DO IT. You will discover a completely new world that will amaze you and give you hundreds of hours of pleasure that you cannot experience in any other way. It will also give you a completely new outlook on life and the way you view it. It will also make you look deep into yourself and analyze your soul. I warn you now, you may not like what you find, but than on the other hand, it may be just what you have always been looking for.

Neptune's Paradise

Here is a 'SCUBBY DOOBY' story. This is what scuba diving is all about. You will not believe me till you try it for yourselves, and I can hear all the Old Divers already saying here comes a load of bullshit and they just might be right but read on and find out for yourselves.

This particular location I am going to describe actually exists. Here is the general location, but you will have to find it for yourselves. After all, I may go back there some day and would like to find it as I remember, and not as some of you 'bottom scratchers' would leave it—RAPED and PILLAGED.

South of California, off the coast of Mexico, there are three very rocky islands in deep water. These three vary small islands form the rough shape of a triangle, and inside the triangle the water is a maximum of about 120 feet deep, whereas the outsides of the islands drop off into very deep water. There are also a series of near vertical cliffs with terraced sandy ledges, giving the appearance of some giant's staircase, and this little island group has to be one of the most beautiful undersea gardens that you will ever see. Some even say it is King Neptune's personal back yard, and if you are ever lucky enough to find it, you will agree. These islands and the surrounding water abound with such a variety of flora and fauna as to be almost unbelievable. The rock cliffs in shallow water are completely covered in a forest of giant California kelp and eel grass that wave continuously in a long, lazy, ground swell that has travelled thousands of miles across the great, blue Pacific Ocean. The sea amongst these islands varies from emerald-green to a near crystal clear aquamarine, filling the canyons, crevasses, tunnels, caves, and archways which make up the bottom contours that you will find throughout the undersea valleys and the floors of these canyons and crevasses that are covered in pure, silver-white sand.

If these islands were totally devoid of all marine life, you could still spend a good part of your lifetime exploring the caves and canyons of this undersea world and never become bored. There is sheer joy in just swimming through the tunnels and canyons, looking at the great archways that look like they were built by the gods themselves as their own cathedrals; a place where the gods come to worship. If you are a religious person, you will never be able to look at man's churches and cathedrals with the same sense of awe as you did before you experienced these undersea valleys of the gods. Man's attempt to build great monuments fade into insignificance when compared to what Mother Nature is capable of producing.

But these islands are not devoid of life. It abounds in such profusion that just to count the species of marine life would take years; as for cataloguing, it would take from now until forever to do so.

The hundreds, maybe thousands of species of fish swimming through the kelp beds are out of this world. Giant sea bass, calicos, sheepshead the size of a small shark, miniature sea horses no longer than your little finger, and everywhere, the bright orange of California's state fish, the Garibaldi. The rocks themselves are covered in abalone, rock scallops, sea urchins, and star fish in every color and hue. The caves and holes are filled with lobsters, giant crabs, and rock dwelling fish, and of course there are the moray eels. These are everywhere, peering from within their lairs, the cracks, and holes in the rocks, sharing their abodes with the ever-present lobsters and crabs.

On the silver sands at the bottom of the canyons and valleys, you will find the sand dollars, sand dabs, and the giant halibuts that weigh as much as 30 and 40 pounds—so many of them you would think that they were holding the world's halibut convention. Mixed in amongst the halibuts, you will find the rays, skates and without looking too hard, you will find the occasional lazy sand shark.

Swimming through the canyons you will spot a giant sea turtle that, if you are lucky and quick enough, you may even be able to hitch a short ride. But to be really lucky, you will spot the most beautiful creature in all the oceans of the world and that is the Giant Manta Ray. This giant black and white, horned ray, with wing tips that can be as much as 20 feet across, glides effortlessly with the slowest movements of its powerful wings. This is one of the most majestic creatures in the ocean. Should you be so lucky to see one of these giant rays, and you don't appreciate the sheer wonder of such a creature, then you are incapable of appreciating anything on this earth.

Of course, the Giant Manta is only one of the majestic creatures in the sea. For you will find just offshore of these islands, the real giants of the oceans. The whales on their annual migration from the northern waters of the Arctic Sea to the southern oceans of the Antarctic which are their summer feeding grounds. When you see one of these huge beasts underwater and realize the beauty with which they grace our oceans, it really makes you wonder how man can continue to slaughter these magnificent mammals. These animals (Maybe they are animals, and then again, maybe they are not animals at all. After all, they have a brain several times larger than our own) must be protected. It's about time that the Japanese, Norwegians, and Russians got their acts together and cease hunting the whale for the small profits they realize. If they don't stop this needless killing, our children will never see a live whale. I appeal to you to do everything in your power to put a stop to this useless slaughter. All right, I will come down off my soap box.

With the whales passing just offshore, it is not uncommon to see another mammal swimming through the shallow waters between the islands. The large California Porpoises. When you see one, there are always several more very close by, but whether these are a family group, or just part of a herd, I don't know. You will have to find out for yourselves. (I wish that I could tell you more about the marine creatures I have encountered in my career, but unfortunately, I'm not a marine biologist. I am just a dumbass deep sea diver, and there are plenty of people who would willingly dispute whether or not there was any truth to that statement, the part about being a DEEP SEA DIVER that is. You wouldn't find a soul to dispute the statement about being a DUMBASS). Porpoises are the other animals on our earth with a brain as large as a man's, and there have been numerous scientific projects over the years attempting to determine just how intelligent these porpoises are. All evidence points to the fact that these creatures are very intelligent, and even appear to have a language that they use to communicate with each other. I would just like to mention that a number of years ago while I was in the Navy, I had an opportunity to work with a "famous" porpoise, and that was an experience of a lifetime. Maybe I will tell you about TUFFY at a later date; he is worth hearing about.

These islands are also used by a large colony of sea lions as breeding grounds, but the seals are the real stars of this underwater world, some would even say the clowns. They can get up to a great deal of mischief underwater, and if your heart is a bit on the weak side, stay away from these islands, for the seals will definitely give you a heart attack. Their favorite trick is to catch you unaware, as they are such fantastic swimmers they seem to appear as if by magic. One moment you will be swimming alone, and the next instant, you will be completely surrounded by a crowd of these clowns, darting and diving straight at you as if they are going to have a head-on collision with you, only to turn away in the very last instant, trailing a stream of bubbles that look like a jet fighter's smoke trail in an aerial display. If this doesn't speed up your old ticker, you are a braver person than me. But the one that always, time after time, gave me a fright, was when I was grubbing in a hole trying to capture a big bug that was just beyond the tips of my fingers, head down, grubbing for all I was worth, only to look up and be face to face with two, huge, glassy eyes less than a foot from my face mask, staring motionless into my eyes. You would be a lucky man during the first second of this close encounter of the third kind, if your bowels didn't release their contents, making it very unpleasant to undress once you had returned to your diving boat. You know your diving buddies would never make any comments to the rest of your friends, regarding the fact that you crapped your drawers just because a little old seal happened to swim in front of you. How could you ever live a disgrace like that down.

Here were the ever-present seals that used the island for their home, darting constantly about performing feats of sheer magic with their swimming abilities. It makes you realize just what a poor undersea creature man is when he is in this unnatural environment. Something like a fish out of water, ungainly, clumsy, awkward, and bulky with all the artificial equipment that he must carry just to breathe, add to that all the other essential gear: wet suit to keep him warm, fins to propel him, gloves for protection, a mask so that he may see the beauty that surrounds him, a compass to guide him so that he doesn't become lost, a depth gauge so he doesn't go too deep and risk the possibility of the dreaded bends, a watch to time his stay, a pressure gauge so that he can monitor his air supply, a large weight belt to compensate for the natural buoyancy of salt water, a goodie bag to place his treasures in, a knife to pry abalone or other shell fish from the rocks, a life vest in case he should get into trouble, and finally, if you are a 'DEEP SEA GREAT WHITE HUNTER', a large, powerful spear gun, preferably with a 12-gauge powerhead to fend off all those man eating creatures that are going to attack and gobble you up. I will tell you right now, 99.9% of the time, if you require a spear gun to protect yourself in the sea, you have no business being there in the first place.

If you have any phobias the ocean will bring them out, so if you are still thinking of becoming a diver, look closely at yourself. If you are afraid of the dark, forget diving as a career as you will spend more time in the water after dark than you ever will in daylight hours—Murphy's Law will make sure of that. If you are afraid of heights, then you don't stand a chance, even though this will not particularly affect you underwater, it certainly will on the surface offshore. They love to place the diving station in the most awkward positions, which are usually as high above the sea as they can get; people love to see divers doing high dives. Are you afraid of animals? I know I don't have to tell you what critters there are in the oceans. What about confined spaces? Do you really believe you can sit inside of a diving bell for eight hours, alone, or swim into an upside-down wreck, or swim into a dark narrow tunnel? If you don't like spiders, you are in a world-of-shit, every creepy crawly in the ocean looks like a spider to some degree, take spider crabs—I assume you will be able to figure out why they got their name without my help. Are you afraid of water? If you are, why the hell are you reading this book? These phobias are not the only ones that will affect you, but they will do for starters. Because I have kept the BIG ONE till last. It is DEATH. Need I say more?

What about your five senses. Some people even say divers need a sixth sense, and I feel we do in fact have a sixth sense. But of the five, your sight is the most important. It lets you see what is going on around you, and lets you appreciate the beauty of this underwater world. Your sense of hearing is also important, although it takes time to realize that there is sound underwater. Most people think it is a silent world, this is not true, the underwater world is in fact noisy—the clicks of the shrimp, the whistles of the porpoises, the bark of seals. Almost every creature in the ocean makes some sort of sound. Then there is the rumble of the waves crashing on the rocks above, causing the clinking and clacking of small, loose rocks caught in the surge; the underwater world is far from being silent. As for your sense of touch, in a great many diving situations, your sense of touch becomes the most important sense of all, even more important than your eyes, because in the dark, black, muddy water your sense of feel becomes your eyes. Not only that, but there is also pleasure in the sense of feel and if you are ever fortunate to touch a seal or a porpoise underwater you will realize what I mean. Taste and smell don't play as an important of a role as the other senses, but they are still there, the taste of salty, slightly fishy seawater leaking around your mouthpiece, and the smell of compressed air from your scuba tanks, all add to the sensations of diving.

What about that sixth sense, you tell me, what is it?

When you are diving and for no apparent reason, the hairs on the nape of your neck stand up, and a cold chill runs down your spine, your hands and lips tremble and you have a feeling that something is watching you, only to turn around to find a 10-foot long, mouth full of teeth, pale as death wolf eel, swimming toward you. If that is not a sixth sense, I will eat page by page the U.S. Navy Diving Manual, the Diver's Bible. Try asking a diver if he thinks he has a sixth sense, and I think you will find 90% of them will. If you get them drunk enough, all of them admit they believe in that important sixth sense.

Unsuitable as man is for the sea, the sea gives him his opportunity to fulfill a dream—a dream that mankind has dreamed since he began losing his tail and first swung down out of the trees (possibly prior to that momentous occasion)—and that is to experience the sensation of flying like the sea gulls soaring and gliding along the cliffs of the islands that are just above the surface of the sea.

I knew I would get to this point sooner or later; here is your chance to soar with the EAGLES, instead of SCRATCHING with the CHICKENS.

Man has many fears, and the fear of heights is one, but when you are underwater, it is easy to overcome this fear in a short time. These islands as I have been describing were in a series of near vertical cliffs dropping off into deep water, an absolutely ideal place to dive. What joy to swim upon one of these sheer cliffs, feeling that tingle of fear as you look over the cliff into an abyss below. And with total abandonment, throw yourself off this cliff and feel that glorious sensation of flying as you control your descent into the depths with the slightest movement of your hand or the arch of your back, to twist and turn down the face of these cliffs, to observe the marine life that dwells in the cracks and crevasses of this fairy tale land, to see the moray eel peering at you with its beady eyes, and to watch the shoals of fish wheeling and dancing in unison only to dart away in fright at your close approach, to soar and glide like an eagle. The joy cannot be described. It must be experienced to understand. This most wonderful sensation of man's—his dreams come true. But as with all things that are truly enjoyable or pleasurable, it's over all too soon and you find yourself too deep and must slowly make your way back towards the surface, the natural environment of man. For all too short of a time, you were able to stray into this alien environment, to enjoy and appreciate, but your own environment beckons to you and you must return immediately or remain forever.

At least, you can have a tremendous amount of pleasure anticipating your next foray into King Neptune's Garden.

On visits to the three islands, we would usually make a two-day trip out of it, so we would spend the night on the rocky shore where we could watch the sea and observe the birds, the seals, and sea lions sporting in the surf. When the sun had finally disappeared into the sea in the West, leaving behind for our pleasure a magnificent sunset, we would prepare a meal of seafood fit for a king. Fresh lobster broiled over an open fire, abalone steaks cooked to perfection, plus many other delicacies of the sea as starters. All these bounties of the sea were washed down by a quantity of excellent sea-cooled white wine. If that is not the perfect ending to an adventure, I don't know what is.

Well, if you are still thinking of becoming a diver and haven't been put off by now, you just may have a chance to join that super elite group known as the PROFESSIONAL DEEP SEA DIVERS, so stand by because I'm going to tell you some of the really interesting and exciting things that happened to these deep sea heroes; it will be sufficient to make you puke, spew, barf, heave your guts out or any other adjectives of a similar nature that you can think of. It will be so rude and nasty that it will make Joan Rivers look like a Mother Superior. So, if you read on from here and get sick, don't blame me, because YOU HAVE BEEN WARNED.

CHAPTER

TWO

Let The Good Times Roll

So now we see, you're a masochist! You were warned and didn't pay heed, so be it. Here we go.

One day on a trip to London, this deep sea diver extraordinaire, a deep diver in more than one sense, as you will see, was asked by his girlfriend to pick up a new vibrator, as hers was shot. So, muff diver, loving fur burgers as much as he did, promised to give it his best to comply with the request of this hot, little piece. He certainly intended to keep her happy. Concluding his business in the early afternoon, with just enough time to get to the airport and catch his plane, he asked the taxi driver if he knew of a sex shop that wasn't too far out of their way. Needless to say, he did; it just happened to be on a busy, main street in Soho.

The taxi driver was able to park just outside the sex shop door on double yellow lines, and told our muff diver that if he hurried, he would wait till he returned. So, 'OLD NO MUFF TOO TOUGH' hurried as quickly as he could so as not to cause any problems for the taxi driver with that Great British institution—the traffic warden.

As 'Muff' rushes into the shop, he spies a dynamite, knock-out, sexy-looking shop assistant, looking at him with a smile on her face. He thinks that she looks very friendly so he rushes over to her and asks if she would assist him, to which she indicated that she would be very pleased to help him and inquired as to what would he be interested in. When Muff said he would like to see the vibrators, she literally beamed then told him she had seen him arrive in a taxi and that he was obviously in a hurry. She now understood why someone would hire a taxi to go to a sex shop, and said she realized what a desperate state MUFF and his girlfriend must have been in when their vibrator malfunctioned!

Speaking of vibrators, here's a "shaky" one for you.

Diver John was well-known (because he told you the moment you first met him) for his unusual sexual tastes.

As John tells the story, he once had a bird, who to most people's way of thinking, could be considered kinky. He said, "There was nothing this TIGRESS didn't know about sex. She was an expert at lowering your chromosome level, and that she gave blowjobs so expertly, she could probably suck the chrome off a trailer hitch. At least she certainly had no problems taking the shine off his knob."

This sex machine had a collection of sex aids and techniques that would make the Happy Hooker's look like a boxful of kiddies' toys. Just to name some—there was rubber, leather, spurs, whips, plastic, vibrators of many sizes, colors and configurations, shackles, goat's eyes, silk, creams and lotions, dildoes from miniatures to gigantic in all the colors of the rainbow, some smooth and shiny, some flaccid, some with large bumps, some soft and furry, and even some with warts. There were gallons of slippery oils and other slimy substances, and of course there were plenty of ropes, straps, chains, silk scarfs, etc. if your bag happened to be bondage. All of this tastefully arranged in an apartment (flat) that looked like it may have been a television studio, considering all the sound recording, video and still camara gear there was just in case you wanted to be a porno star in your very own production.

It has just occurred to me that if you had a flair for making porn films and were a diver, an appropriate title would be *DIVERS DO IT DEEPER*, or if you were a cowboy, *COWBOYS STAY IN THE SADDLE LONGER* or if you were a welder, *WELDERS HAVE HOTTER RODS*. How about a truck driver, *FUCKING TRUCKING*. If you happen to be a Lorry Driver, I think you are a bit out of luck.

As you can see, this lady took her sexual pleasures seriously, and she wasn't even a pro, just a gifted amateur, so says John, who enjoyed her sexual pleasures.

As the rest of the story goes, as John was partaking of the sexual delights this sex machine had to offer late one evening, experimenting, with one of her less exotic toys—a common or ordinary everyday garden variety vibrator. Seemingly, during a moment of overwhelming passion, Sweetmeat became carried away and stuffed this instrument of sexual pleasure right up John's posterior end, where to both of their shocked surprise, it completely disappeared.

They tried a few old home remedies to remove this shaking foreign object from John's shit chute i.e. a jar of Vaseline, a tube of K.Y. jelly and a quart of Wesson Oil. They even tried the old stand-by, the plumber's helper, all to no avail.

The only recourse left was a trip to their local hospital for a visit to the Emergency Ward. I will not even attempt to describe what took place in the hospital. The questions of how, why, when, where etc. I will leave to your imagination. Can you imagine all those sly grins, little giggles behind raised hands, and uproarious belly busting laughs behind closed doors. Think of the expressions on the faces of all those trainee nurses and young interns!

Do you know what John's comments to this whole affair were? It went something along the lines of "Screw Duracell, I will buy cheap batteries for the rest of my life, the whole night was a shaking experience, and I didn't receive one good vibration in that hospital."

Only Human

I met a diver offshore one time that kept referring to himself as a 'masturbating pig.' When I asked him why he called himself the masturbating pig, he told me this story:

It appeared that he had relationship problems with his new mother-in-law, and as all the mother-in-law stories go, she seemingly couldn't stand him, and would never forgive her daughter for taking up with a deep sea diver in the first place. As he tells it, she must have had a bad experience with a diver in her youth to have hated divers as much as she hated him.

His wife of a few months wanted him and his mother-in-law to kiss and make up so she arranged for her parents to spend a weekend with them. He agreed to these arrangements with tribulation but told his wife that he would give it his best shot to please her and would make a real effort to try and get along with her mother.

The big day finally arrived, and he greeted her parents upon their arrival at their house for the weekend. He said, "You talk about cold; my mother-in law's look would have frozen the balls off that brass monkey," but as he had promised his new bride to be that he would try to please her mother, he invited them into their home. The atmosphere was so thick that you could cut it with a knife, so he knew that the only thing to do was offer them a drink and hope the alcohol would work its old magic and make the weekend bearable.

After a few Harvey Wallbangers (you will find why they are so named in Chapter VIII) he said she was actually smiling at him, and it looked like everything was going to turn out alright after all.

His wife prepared a stupendous dinner while he continued to ply them with an assortment of drinks: pre-dinner cocktails, sherry with the hors d' oeuvres, white wine with the starter, red wine with the main course, a sweet white snow wine with dessert, port with the cheese, then coffee and a number of different, fine liqueurs. He said that by the time they retired to the living room that he had her parents so well oiled that they were definitely not feeling any pain.

Over his finest bottle of cognac, his mother-in-law had begun to ask him questions regarding life offshore, at which time he felt that he had really cracked it.

After a couple of hours, she finally got around to asking that one question that every person who has never been offshore wants to know the answer to: . . . what do young, healthy men do about their sex life OFFSHORE? After all, being away from female companionship for several months at a time is not necessarily a normal thing. Our fearless diver, himself having indulged in a bit too much of the nectar of the grapes by this time, thought to himself, *Ah, that closed mind of hers is finally seeing the light and is opening up to the real world.*

He decided that now that she has seen the light, he would tell her the truth so he told her, "Most of the men, when they feel the urge, masturbate." She looked at him for a moment, then enquired if he used this method of sexual relief himself. To which our brave, fearless superhero replies, "I am only human."

He went on to explain that he had never seen a women move so fast in his life as she grabbed her husband by the arm and headed for the door, shouting, "COME ON! I will not spend another second in this house with that MASTURBATING PIG."

Our hero finished his tale with, "That was five years ago, and I have not seen her since, and that is why I call myself the MASTURBATING PIG, to make sure I don't forget. In case she shows up again, I will know precisely how to get rid of her." Maybe that's something to keep in mind if you have mother-in-law problems.

Fake It, Till You Make It

There was a small diving company that found themselves in need of a man to be a driver, clean the shop, and in general look after things.

The wheel (BOSS) interviewed several young lads until he found a likely candidate for this glamorous job. The young man was hired and turned out to be a good lad, always did as he was requested, and was keen to get on with all the men working in the shop.

In this shop, they had installed a decompression chamber just in case one of the divers should get the dreaded bends and require recompression for treatment.

Over the next few months, it was noticed that there began to appear a line of small stars on the decompression chamber. There was speculation as to who, and why, these stars were being painted onto the chamber.

Then late one evening, one of the divers who had made a deep dive late in the afternoon, began suffering pain from expanding gas bubbles (that is what the dreaded bends are all about). He called a couple of the other divers and asked them to meet him at the shop as he was suffering some discomfort and needed some treatment (This little ploy also works well if you wanted to get away from the old lady, for a piss-up with the boys). When they arrived at the shop and were getting ready to set the chamber up, they noticed that there was already someone inside, and on closer inspection what did they find, but our stalwart, young lad in the chamber with a young bird, balling their brains out.

Anyway, they threw a bucket of cold water, or whatever it is you do to break-up a copulating couple, got them out of the chamber, and on their way. They then treated the bent diver (I don't mean "BENT" as in kinky). After a couple of hours, he was alright and they retired to the local bar for some much needed liquid refreshment where the 'handy dandy shop cleaner' was drowning his sorrow because his bird had flown the coop after realizing that he, in fact, was not a deep sea diver as he had portrayed himself to be.

So, the whole story came out how our lad had been making a nightly round of all the bars, chatting up the chicks, telling them he was a rough, tough, deep sea diver, and taking them back to the shop to show them the decompression chamber and other diving gear, and every time he scored, he painted another star onto the side of the chamber just like a World War II fighter pilot. And I can tell you, if the number of stars painted onto that chamber is any indication, that lad is a REAL ACE.

Here is another story along the same lines, I guess an appropriate name for this story would be, *WOULD YOU LIKE TO "COME" RIDE IN MY YELLOW SUBMARINE?*

Like I have said in the past, divers are natural born exhibitionists, many of them have no qualms about baring all, or even putting on a performance for the viewing pleasure of their fellow diving buddies.

The episodes in this story took place on several different occasions, about ten years ago. And as I have mentioned on many occasions, divers are clever, sly, and devious characters. You will see by this story just how true those words prove to be. This story would almost be more appropriate in guerilla theater than in this chapter, but whether it's right or wrong, here it is, and here it is going to stay.

Amateur Performance

I don't want to wish any bad luck on any of the divers involved, but if any of the females that were involved read this, there are undoubtedly going to be a few divers around with black eyes— that's if they are lucky. If they are unlucky, they may WIND-UP DEAD. What can be more terrible to behold than the unleashed fury of a mistreated and deceived female?

How do I start this tale? How about with some background on how submarines are (in this case, I should say were) used in the offshore commercial diving industry.

These were the days before the widespread use of ROV (Remote Operated Vehicles) to do inspection work, like pipelines or platforms. This is where the small mini subs came into their own and were used to fly the pipelines making a video recording for the oil companies, or diver's inspection of the offshore structures. These submarines were built with two compartments, one that remained at surface pressure for the pilot and observer, and the other compartment could be pressurized to bottom depth so that one or more divers could lock out to do useful work on bottom. At the time, these subs were top-line technology in the diving industry, and most divers wanted to be part of a submarine crew.

Anytime that one of the motherships came into harbor, it drew a great deal of attention as all the people associated with the diving game wanted to have a look at this new attraction in the diving world.

It only stood to reason that the divers would pick up on this unique center of attraction to attract the ladies and this they did and used to their immense satisfaction in more ways than one.

There would be a party on board every night after the pubs closed. You see, those deep sea divers would hit the beach telling all those poor innocent (sic) little girls what big, macho divers they were and were inviting all these sweet dolly birds back to the ship for free drinks, a wild party, and a chance to look at their pretty, little, yellow submarine. What sweet thing could resist a line like that?

Well, after plying these innocent, little girls with copious quantities of their favorite plonk, and the sweet thing of the moment was in a receptive mood, one of the divers would invite his lovely to take that promised look at their little yellow submarine.

As soon as the diver and his lovely had departed the party, the rest of the divers and in-the-know crowd would duly make their way to the dive control room where the television monitor would be switched on and the video recorder would be made ready for a recording of the "UP-COMING" performance.

Needless to say, the television camera normally used to record the pipeline would have previously been turned around so that it would give a good field of view of all things that would be happening inside the submarine. This crew of deviate voyeurs would then sit back sipping a glass of chilled wine and enjoy an uncensored, live performance of eroticism which would have brought tears to the eyes of the HAPPY HOOKER, otherwise known as pure, wanton, carnal fornication, with the sounds of lust issuing from the speakers. These shameless deep sea divers enjoyed their voyeurism and recorded for future enjoyment while offshore on those cold, winter evenings the scene of copulation that was happening before their very eyes.

The Backfiring Bellyflop

Are divers exhibitionists? I personally would call anyone who could even get it up, let alone perform in a yellow submarine with a crowd of lecherous divers watching, an exhibitionist.

To answer your question, "YES!" Divers are exhibitionists, they will drop their pants at the drop of a hat. This act is normally known as 'dropping trou' and depending on the circumstances, an exhibitionist may earn a great many HERO POINTS, providing that he executes his performance in such a manner as to cause the maximum amount of surprise and shock. These HERO POINTS, of course, are awarded by his fellow divers, in the form of envy and admiration.

Of course, timing is everything when attempting such a stunt, and if he should fail to pull off his stunt for some reason, he then loses a large percentage of the points that he has accumulated in the past and becomes an object of ridicule, from his peers, because divers, probably more so than most folk, are unable to tolerate ineptitude.

Big George was an 'exhibitionist extraordinary', but as you will be able to see by this tale, without proper thought and planning, even an 'exhibitionist extraordinary' can come unstuck.

In the oil capital of Britain, there is a hotel owned by one of the world-renowned hotel chains that has a swimming pool located adjacent to the bar which is very handy indeed for watching the dolly birds in their most fetching swimwear. And, as we all know, swimming pools and man's favorite drink known as alcohol do not mix particularly well together. Where have you ever been where there is a pool and strong beverages, and where someone didn't get chucked into the drink?

I can assure you that this hotel was no exception. There was hardly an evening that passed that some high-spirited, amorous lover didn't rearrange his lady love's hairdo with a good, old-fashioned dunking, or a bunch of drunks didn't heave another drunk into the deep six.

The staff of this reputable establishment looked on these high-spirited charades with total indifference, with a bored look on their faces as if to say, "I have seen it all before" which in reality, was about a hundred times a month.

Big George and a crowd of his mates were partaking of some liquid refreshment in this urbanized boozer one evening, bragging about themselves, telling lies and just having a good old bull-shit session, interspaced with numerous cheers, bottom ups, down the hatch, skol, prost, sla'inte, here's-mud-in-your-eye, etc. At this fast and furious pace, it wasn't very long before these gentlemen reached a pleasant state of intoxication, known as 'pleasantly pissed' which a diver would more likely refer to as shit-faced.

Big George, having become slightly inebriated and growing bored with the stimulating conversation, decided it was time to create a little excitement by a performance of exhibitionism. No sooner having made his decision, Big George went into action by 'dropping trou', giving one and all a 'brown eye' shot, then stripping to his birthday suit and casually strolling across the bar balls ass naked where he executed a perfect belly flop into the swimming pool.

Big George pops to the surface expecting to find the bar in a state of pandemonium, only to find that there has not been one decibel of change in the background noise level. Not one person was paying the slightest bit of attention to Big George. As far as he could tell, there was not even one eyebrow raised in outrage. You could almost see the cogs turn in his alcohol befuddled brain, *What the hell's gone wrong, I should be a hero* and as he realized that no one was going to pay him any attention, that there was not going to be any surprise or shock and his performance was a flop; Big George's bravado turned to embarrassment, starting at pretty pink and turning rapidly to raging red.

I have mentioned the impermeability of the hotel staff, and now they put it to maximum effect, for they let Big George stew in his own juices, standing there in the middle of the pool without a stitch of clothes on, until he felt like the lowest of the low, and finally one of the hotel porters came to Big George's rescue, with what can only be described as "class."

As he stood holding a large, fluffy towel for Big George to cover himself in, he enquired in a polite, dignified voice that should have been on the stage, for his voice carried crystal clear to the far corners of that packed bar, "DID YOU ENJOY YOUR SWIM, SIR?"

That statement had the effect that Big George had unsuccessfully attempted. It brought the house down.

The last thing I have to say is that porter was one of those people who are few and far between—he had "THE RIGHT STUFF."

Now you know the truth! Divers can make mistakes (But not very often)! There is an old saying: "show me a diver that has never made a mistake, and I will show you a diver that has never done anything."

The Bathroom Scales

There were six slightly overweight divers sitting in their local one afternoon, quaffing pints of beer like they were going out of fashion (did I say slightly overweight? What I meant to say was there were six, fat divers sitting in a pub). As with any conversation that lasts over five minutes, the subjects of diets and being overweight cropped up, with each of the divers admitting that he may be a little overweight but always justifying this statement with "It's not what I eat, it's just the beer".

As these chubby 'deep sea divers extraordinaire' continued to consume large quantities of barley wine, their calorie intake increased, and so did their courage, 'Dutch courage' in this instance, as the brew flowed so did that warm feeling of invincibility, until the challenge of a dieting contest became irresistible to these fearless heroes.

With the challenge accepted by all, the only thing left to decide were the ground rules. It was agreed that the stakes were to be $200 dollars per man and the contest would be over 30 days winner-take-all. There was the stipulation that the winner had to buy all the beer that the five losers could drink on the day that the contest finished. By this time, there were not many patrons of this pub that didn't know what was going on, which seems reasonable considering that divers are not noted for their quiet conversations. Since the divers couldn't come to an agreement on who would hold the money, as they did not trust each other with the pot, it was finally agreed that the bar owner, Louie and his wife, Marlene, would hold the stakes and be the official referees, starting at this very minute with the Official Weigh-in.

Marlene brought out her bathroom scales, which were to be the Official Scales for the contest. After the contestants were satisfied with the scales, each diver weighed in turn, with his name and weight being duly recorded by the officials. They were to have the final weigh-in at noon exactly 30 days hence. Thus, with all details ironed out, these contestants got down to some serious drinking as this was the last chance of a drink for thirty days.

Well, after thirty long, dry, days the big day finally arrived, our 'fat divers' all arrived with great expectations. Two of them with the expectation of being $200 dollars richer, and four of them expecting to get as drunk as they could on the $200 dollars each that they were donating to the cause as they had found out that their will power was not as strong without the 'Dutch courage.' They had deluded themselves into thinking they would prevail on that fateful day thirty days previous when they let their alligator mouth overload their hummingbird assholes.

As the divers arrived, so did a large portion of their friends, sensing that there was going to be a good time had by all, plus there was a chance that they may get in on some of the free beer that was bound to be flowing.

The time for the Official Weigh-in had arrived, four of the divers didn't stand a chance, and so conceded defeat, leaving the other two to determine who would be the "undisputed weight losing champion."

Now I ask you? What are the chances of two 'deep sea divers extraordinaire' losing exactly the same amount of weight over a thirty-day period? The odds must be hundreds if not thousands to one, but that is precisely what happened. And this did not make one of the divers happy as he thought that he had a sure thing and was not well-disposed to split the money with the other diver, but he did eventually agree that it was a dead heat and the money was split between the two and the party began.

The booze flowed freely as predicted, and everybody was enjoying themselves; our unhappy diver kept talking about the fact that he thought he had lost more weight that the other diver. Then, he decided that his clothes must have been the reason that he weighed more than he expected to have weighed. So, (Yes, you are right) off comes all his clothes to reweigh himself. Marlene, hearing all the excitement that this act caused, came around the bar to see what was going on. When she saw our exhibitionist extraordinary in all his glory, she burst into hysterical laughter, with tears running down her cheeks and proclaimed, ". . . have you ever seen such a big man with such a little thing."

Well, it goes without saying, our "big diver" didn't have nearly as good of a day as he thought he was going to have when he got out of bed that morning.

CHAPTER

THREE

Their Women

The setting is a small hotel named the Crowing Cock in Scotland, well noted for it's lenient drinking hours which is ideal for the offshore, North Sea hands that like to truly enjoy themselves. You could find a crowd of piss artists anytime, night or day, raising hell, telling lies, and getting absolutely shit-faced drunk. It was truly an 'oil patch' bar with an international flavor; there were Dutch, Norwegian, Germans, Spanish, Danes, Swedes, Scots, Sassenachs, and always a large, boisterous crowd of American Coon-asses and Texans. (I can hear them Yanks now, "Hey, Bartender, give me a whisky, and I don't mean that rotgut shit you call whisky, I want bourbon and a little splash of branch," or "Don't y'all have any Jack Daniels or Southern Comfort" or "When I say, I want ice in my drink, I MEAN ICE, not one of those little, bitty pieces no bigger than a butterbean)."

Where there are oil field hands you will always find their women. These ladies are after only a few simple things in life: first and uppermost is to just have a good time, second most important is a good Sugar Daddy who loves to spend all his hard-earned bucks (or whatever currency he is paid) on partying, booze, gold, a few diamonds, other rare gems and thrown in just for good measure, fine clothes, and luxurious living. She also likes the finer things in life—for instance, dining in very expensive restaurants, sipping champagne, plus flying first class to exotic places around the world like Hawaii, Bali, or the Bahamas. It is not absolutely necessary, but a long, low, fast, sports job, hand built in Wopland, helps to sweeten the pie (and I don't mean apple pie or any other type of pie you have in mind, what I mean is 'hair pie', see glossary for definition).

It never ceases to amaze me what a hard cock will do to an otherwise rational man's mind. His common sense seems to desert him completely. He will do anything that that piece of tail asks of him, including complying with all the things I have listed above that her wicked heart desires. The only thing I can figure is that when a man gets an erection, it must be the lack of a sufficient quantity of blood reaching his brain cells to sustain a logical thought process.

On his week, two weeks, or whatever time he gets ashore for some time off, he spends every red cent that he worked his ass off to earn on his last trip offshore on that lovely little piece of ass that has been telling him what a great big handsome hunk of man he is and how much she loves him and always will because he is the only man that ever satisfied her.

After he has run out of money and sobers up enough to realize that he is already several days overdue back at work, 'sweet thing' drives him to the docks in that fantastic, Italian, go-faster car. He catches a boat that he will have to ride for forty hours to get to the job site in a storm force 11, puking his guts out all the way.

He will, for the first few hours, be so sick that he is afraid that he is going to die, and the rest of the trip so sick that he's afraid that he is NOT going to die. Just before he boards the supply boat, she gives him a few lovin' little gropes and swears never ending love for him (this is just to make sure that he doesn't forget his promise that he would send her his paycheck as soon as he gets it, so she can pay the house rent and get his favorite brand of booze stocked up before he comes ashore three months from now).

After a final kiss and a tearful goodbye, she promises that she will keep the little fur burger that he loves so much warm just for him. He finally boards the boat, and she remains at the dockside waving to him till the vessel clears the harbor wall and disappears from sight.

She then jumps into his/her wopmobile, launches into orbit without ground clearance, straight back to their/her flat that he so lavishly furnished with nothing but the best. She admires the huge video screen, turns on the laser disc quadrophonic multi-thousand pound sound system that she convinced him the day before yesterday that they must have if they were going to entertain his friends properly, and pours herself a tall, refreshing drink from a stocked bar that looks like it has been transplanted from the London Hilton.

Relaxing while sipping her gin and tonic, she thinks to herself, *Now what am I going to do with myself for the next three months.* As she muses over these thoughts, she finally decides that the best way to handle problems like these are to take them one day at a time. So, let's see: *the first thing I will do is have a long hot soak in the bath with lots of bubbles,* then *what will I wear, Oh, the men really like that black low-cut sexy dress he bought for me last week, yes that, and lots of jewelry. And that perfume he brought me from the duty-free shop his last trip ashore, what's the name of it? Oh yes, Chanel No. 5, not Charrol*

*Number Five as that stupid ass calls it, then down to the Cunt and Cock;
oh! that's not right, it's the Crowing Cock; oh! that sounds almost like
'growing cock' and that's just what I need right now.*

So, as we can see, 'sweet thing' has solved her dilemma of what
to do with herself for the next three months, just like she and her
'sisters of kind', have been doing since man lived in caves and had
to go hunting dangerous critters in order to bring home the bacon.

The only thing I have to say about the above tale is that it
doesn't happen just to deep sea divers. And if there are some of
you gents that say to yourselves, *That has never happened to me,*
you better go see your local shrink because you definitely have a
problem with your memory. If the shrink checks you out O.K.,
then I would say that you have a very much more serious problem,
you are undoubtedly a fruit.

This one took place a number of years ago on the West Coast
of California.

Doc had been married a number of years to a really nice girl;
they had two or three little tricycle motors, a nice home, and were
still in love after all these years. His wife was well-known for her
good sense of humor, Doc normally worked close to home, and so
was able to be home most nights which suited his wife just fine.

On this particular occasion, Doc had taken a little diving job
that was about 400 miles from his home and would only be there
for a couple of weeks, plus he would be able to come home for the
weekends.

It turned out, as with most diving jobs, that one ran several
weeks longer than expected. By which time, Doc was fed up with
driving into the early hours of Saturday morning, spending what
only seemed like minutes with his family, and then driving all
those miles back on Sunday to arrive bleary-eyed and then have to

dive all day. The way Doc put it, "It feels like that goddamn Bug (Volkswagen) has grown to my ass."

That week, California suffered extremely bad weather, gale force winds, rain, floods, power lines were blown down, there were mud slides, and bridges were washed out. Doc had made up his mind that that he was not going to spend all this weekend driving in weather like this just for a few hours at home, so he decided to call his wife and tell her he was going to spend the weekend with the other divers at the motel and he would see her the following weekend.

So, Friday after work, the other divers were sitting in the motel bar waiting for Doc to join them for a drink after he had finished phoning his wife, when one of them looked out of the window and saw Doc throwing his gear into the Bug. Of course, they had to find out what was going on so out they went to Doc's car where he was just finishing cramming the Bug full of gear and asked him what was going on, to which Doc replied, "When I told my wife that I was spending the weekend with you guys, and that I wasn't going to drive in weather like this just for a few hours at home," she said, "It was O.K. with her but, come midnight, there was going to be some screwing and if I wanted in on it, I had better be there."

Wayne's "Miracle" Cure

Here is a "quickie."

Wayne who always was a bit weird anyway had been told by some backroom quack that if you urinated on your feet, it would prevent athlete's foot. Wayne's wife, entering the bathroom one day, noticed that Wayne was in the shower applying this prophylactic medication for the prevention of athlete's foot. When she asked him what he was doing, he said, "Pissing on my feet." With a look of puzzlement, becoming enlightenment, she finally replied, ". . . what ever turns you on."

And you wonder why people think divers are kinky!

Back in Europe and the North Sea:

While offshore, the barge that we were working on suffered mechanical problems with its large crane, and it was necessary to come into a harbor to effect repairs.

We arrived in Amsterdam, the diamond capital of the world, hit the beach for a run ashore, returned to the barge the next day to be told by the captain that it was going to require a week to ten days to complete the repairs to the crane, and since the diving crew would not be required, we were free to do as we pleased, as long as we checked in every couple of days so he would know where to find us if anything came up.

The divers packed their gear and headed downtown to a small hotel that's located near Canal Street and had always made us welcome in the past, checked in, called our wives/mistresses/lovers/girlfriends/or our favorite female companion of the moment, and asked them to join us for a week of good times in Amsterdam.

In due course, these lovely creatures arrived, were settled into the hotel, and introduced to each other and surprise, surprise, they actually managed to get along together quite well. So, for the first couple of days, there was much merriment and good times had by all. Of course, the girls/birds finally got around to comparing notes, talking about clothes, fur coats and, of course, gold and diamonds.

Rita who was a Scot, but you would think Irish (as you will see), was going with one of the divers who was Norwegian and believe it or not had a heart of gold (maybe that was what she was after). Anyway, during these female chats, Rita realized that she was the only one of the sweet things that didn't have a diamond ring.

Well, with threats, friendly persuasion, or whatever wily methods these creatures use to get their way, our Norwegian friend went out and bought Rita a very large, solitaire, diamond ring, costing several thousands of dollars, came back to the hotel and presented this beautiful diamond to Rita in front of the whole crowd of us. I swear I nearly shit (it looked like something Richard would buy for Liz). That rock was so big that if Rita fell into one of the many canals in Amsterdam, she was surely going to drown.

We could tell for some reason that Rita was not pleased with the ring (It was most likely her bitching, that she didn't like it, and wanted one with a lots of diamonds). Well, to make a long story short, Jarle took the ring back and got her one that she wanted—just like the other girls were wearing—one with lots of little diamonds.

Jarle, with a big shit-eating grin, said, ". . . that suited him, that ring only cost about a tenth of what the other one cost."

A Woman's Tender Love And Car

I wonder if that story has anything to do with female logic? Here is one that demonstrates just how logical and analytical the female mind is.

This diver who lived in Aberdeen, Scotland, and looked almost like myself, so let's call him, Bill, had a wife that resembled my lovely wife almost to a "T", so let's call her, Karen. (You don't really think I would tell a story about my wife's logic, or lack of?).

Karen had been bitching to Bill that she wanted a new car, so Bill being a nice guy, decided to splurge and buy Karen a new Triumph Stag, the car of most young wives' dreams (I think it's because they visualize themselves driving down a country lane with the top down, birds singing, the sun shining, and the wind blowing through their hair. Also, there was a commercial on the telly along those lines that may have something to do with giving these young ladies such ideas).

The car was ordered and Karen and Bill began making plans to take a motoring holiday when the car arrived. Karen's father, who is a very keen motorist, told Karen all the pertinent things that she needed to know about how to break-in a new car (run in)—all the do's and all the don'ts.

Finally, the car arrived and with 00000.9 miles on the clock, Karen and Bill set off to see the sights in the south of England in that shiny, new sports car. Of course, Karen insisted that Bill drive so as to be sure that the car was properly run in. Let me assure you that by the time the car had 00001.9 miles on the clock, Karen was telling Bill that he was mistreating her new car because her father had explained all the do's and don'ts to her.

Two weeks later and over 2000 miles on the clock, Karen and Bill were on their way home, and like most of us when you get ready to go home, you can't wait to get there. So, Bill had the bit between his teeth and was unlimbering that Stag down the motorway, listening to the quiet, smooth purr of that V-8 engine. He really could listen because Karen hadn't said a word for the last hour. When Bill asked her what was wrong, she said not a word. She just sat there, with a look of determination on her face. An hour and a half later, nearing their home, Bill asked her again what was bothering her, and this time she replied, "You have been mistreating my car but that's O.K. because I am going to drive it at 40 miles per hour for the next month to make up for the damage that you have done to it."

The only thing I can figure out was that with her female logic she thought that a machine was like a sick dog or cat that you could nurse it back to health with tender loving care.

A Good Time

Speaking of animals, divers are normally referred to as animals and rightfully so, but you wouldn't believe what some of the women that associated with these fine gentlemen can be like—animal would just not be a strong enough adjective. You think divers have a colorful way of speaking, well let me assure you, some of their women could put a mule skinner to shame; they know swear words that haven't even been invented yet, and even with the words that we all know and love, they have a way of using them that sheds a completely new light on the meaning of swear words.

Have you ever heard a woman call a man a mother fucker? I mean when she says mother fucker it comes out MOTHER FUCK-ER. Or how about COCK SUCK-ER; it must be how they place the emphasis on those heavy "K" sounds, I mean they really accent them. Try saying one of the nasties above, placing the accent on the "K"s and see if you understand what I'm referring too.

The only reason I broached this subject is that it just didn't seem fair to leave out all those women who showed us a good time when we were down on our luck. No diving job, far away from home and loved ones, they listened to our sob stories held our hands, and in most cases laid a little pussy on us to soothe our poor hurt pride or whatever. You do know who I'm talking about? Oh, don't tell me you have forgotten? Remember? Rosey Rottencrotch, Slack Alice, Juicy Lucy, Diamond Lil, Tool Tootin' Tresh, Syphilitic Syl, and everybody remembers Penicillin Penny, the Queen of the SILVER DOLLAR and that it took two million units or more just to cure the loving she laid on you. Hell, I had better stop there, because if I continue it would upset my wife if she thought that I knew them all. But, of course, in my case she knows that they only listened to my sob stories.

Reminiscing like this reminds me of a story that an old diver told me about the finest piece of ass he ever had.

He had been on a diving job in some godforsaken place out past beyond, no female companionship for over a year—nothing but old lady thumb and her four daughters. Then one day, his diving boat broke down and he drifted into the beach where low and behold what did he spy—a FEMALE, a real live FEMALE. He said "She twern't much to look at, but boy, oh boy, she sure had some good pussy." He went on to tell me in great detail just how ugly she really was; *it was enough to make you puke*, I thought, *until* *he finally got around to telling about this fine piece of pussy.* He said, "She really had a big pussy, but it didn't matter because on one side of her labium she had warts, and on the other side, she had worm holes and all you had to do was stick your cock into that slimy cunt and snap the warts into the worm holes until you got a perfect fit." If after that, you've still got your lunch and are looking forward to dinner, and you are not a diver already, you are definitively diver material. NOTE* If you believe this one is true, there is no hope for you.

The Straw That Broke The Diver's Back

There was a fairly young English diver working in the North Sea that seemed to always have wife problems; he had been married for a number of years to what I can only think must have been a highly strung, or neurotic lady. The reason I say that is every time Bob would go offshore in the course of six or eight weeks, he would receive a number of phone calls from his missus about some crisis that she was unable to cope with. It seems this lady was always going to the doctor with imagined problems such as the kids were sick when in reality there was not a thing wrong with them; the car was always broken down, even when it was new and the house was ready to fall down, and so it went.

Poor Old Bob lived in a constant state of turmoil, not knowing when to expect that next call, but knowing for sure it was just around the corner.

Over a period of several years, Bob continued to live under his paranoid wife. On several occasions, she convinced him that he must be home to look after her and her problems, and Bob would make all the arrangements for a relief to go home and sort things out.

Bob would finally arrive back on the job after losing several weeks of work just to nip home and expect to be back in a few days to take up where he left off. It does not work that away. To begin with, it costs a company a great deal of money to transport you to the job site and they sure as hell are not going to hire someone else for a few days and move them with all the expenses involved, just so you can nip off home for a dirty weekend (That's assuming that you ever get back onto that job at all). These diving companies take a dim view of people they feel they can't rely on; after one or two times of having to leave the job before your contract is complete, they say to hell with you, we will get someone we know will stay till the job is completed. Anyway, Bob would arrive back and explain that it was one more false alarm, that she had made up 99% of the problems just to get him home to nag and bitch at him.

Bob really loved the diving business, and it was the only thing that he really wanted to do, and was the only thing he was trained to do. Bob had wanted to go to the beach and take another job, but he couldn't do in addition to supporting his wife and family in the manner to which they were accustomed.

Over a number of years, you could see Bob and his wife growing slowly more and more apart until it finally reached the point of no return. As the story goes, Bob's wife is one of those people who just can't stand to be by themselves, and had finally found herself a boyfriend, and as is always the case, the husband/ wife is the last one to know.

In short, when Bob finally learned that his wife was having an affair, it was too late to do anything about it as it was now well past the point of no return. So, his wife filed for a divorce, and Bob found himself a little dolly bird in Scotland.

In due course, the divorce proceedings were completed and Bob learned how he had come out on the deal.

With alimony and child support, his ex-wife received about 90% of all Bob earned; she got all their savings, and the rest of the deal didn't look all that good either.

Well, this made Bob just a little unhappy so he decided that he would make a trip to England to discuss these arrangements with his ex-wife. When Bob arrived, he found his ex-wife living with her boyfriend in what used to be his home but she was very understanding. She understood perfectly how she had taken him to the cleaners; she laughed at him and told him she didn't understand what he was so upset about. After all, he received half of everything, it was a 50/50 split; she got the house, he got the payments; she got car, he got the payments; she got the furnishings, he got the payments, and so on.

Well, you might think as the old saying goes this was the last straw and you would be absolutely right. Bob lost his nut and said he would split everything down the middle for her; Bob went out of what used to be his house into what used to be his garage, got what used to be his chainsaw, and went back into the house and proceeded to divide everything down the middle—the dining room table, along with the chairs, the living room sofa, the television, and so on right throughout the whole house until he came to her wardrobe. This he left intact, saying, she would need that to keep her half of her nice clothes in (Have you ever seen what a chainsaw can do to a closet full of frilly dresses?).

Bob's parting shot was, "you can send my half to the salvation army."

When we asked Bob what his ex-wife's boyfriend did during this uproar, Bob just looked at us as if we had a screw loose and said, "what would you do?" Now I ask you, what would you do?

Considering that you are standing face to face with a pissed-off diver with a chain saw in his hands . . .

Slippery George

Here is another story along the same lines, but this time the shoe is on the other foot.

George was one of those types of guys that are never going to get married. No matter what happens, he will live with a bird forever and promise her the moon without any intention of ever keeping one word of his promises. As our story unfolds, we find George living with his girlfriend; they were now into about their fourth year together. In their case, she was the one furnishing the nest, she had bought everything in their rented flat, including the carpet on the floor and the drapes on the walls.

Our heroine had been onto George for the last year or so to get married, but Old George was being as slippery as humanly possible. During some of our after-work pub sessions, George took great delight in telling his latest method of, as he put it, 'escaping the hangman's noose.'

Of course, most of these methods were of the sly and devious type. Well, as we all watched with great interest, we knew deep in our hearts Old George was skating on thin ice, because no matter how sly and devious a man may think he is, he can't hold a candle to a woman when it comes right down to the nut cutting.

Well, George held out a hell of a lot longer than we ever thought he could. And I guess in the end you could even say that George won, (George's favorite saying was "skill will overcome the untrained mind every time," but I will leave that decision to you).

George returned home late one evening to their rented flat after a heavy drinking session with the boys, inserted his key into the lock and opened the door to find that there was not a thing left in the flat, including the carpet on the floors and the drapes on the walls. Seems our heroine suffered enough of Old George's promises and had a moving company in that day and moved her out. As the old saying goes, lock, stock and barrel. George, being too drunk to even go check into a hotel, spent a very long night sleeping on those cold bare floors with nothing but his conscience for company.

The next day when all of George's mates heard that George was once again truly a bachelor, they decided to do something to show their friendship towards Old George.

Seeing as how George was stuck with an empty flat, a care package seemed like the most appropriate way of showing George they really cared.

A large poster was drawn up, depicting George's situation, and giving very descriptive details on the causes of his unfortunate circumstances, appealing to all of George's friends to give generously, anything they could spare to make George's empty flat into some semblance of a home. These posters were hung in every conspicuous place that could be found in the office.

It was wonderful how George's friends in his time of need came to the rescue. It brings a tear to my eye every time I remember their generosity. There was an old moth-eaten army blanket, one large beat-up black pot with a bag of beans, a cracked teacup with a bent teaspoon and two tea bags, a large stack of porno magazines and most important of all there was Beryl, his very own blow-up rubber doll.

So, there you have it, his friends responded to all of George's needs. They had given George warmth and substance for his body;

literature, for his mind (food for thought?); and companionship, for his soul.

The moral of this story: there is nothing in the world that is a substitute for real friendship.

What happened to George's girlfriend? The last we heard, one of George's friends saw her at the airport with a doctor, on their way to Monte Carlo for their honeymoon.

C H A P T E R
FOUR

The Things They Do

It's very hard to differentiate between the things divers do offshore, and the things they get up to on the beach.

This chapter will be in a very similar nature to "LET THE GOOD TIMES ROLL," but these happenings take place offshore rather than on the beach; maybe they will be fun, maybe they won't.

I will let you be the judge of that.

Every time I think of diving jobs and divers, I always think of the first day when you are mobilizing. There is everyone showing up in buses, taxis, on foot, by one-eyed jackasses, Rolls-Royces, bicycles, wopmobiles, and one time I saw a diver show up on a skateboard—you name it and it will be there. And almost every one of these hands will be in varying states of intoxication, some staggering, stumbling drunk, and some past that stage, I mean like crawling. I even saw a guy passed out, with his mate pushing him in a wheelbarrow that he had stolen for that purpose.

But that's not what strikes me as odd. What really gets you are the differences in dress appearances. There is the American pipeline welder—he will be dressed from head to foot as a cowboy. He will be wearing a Stetson cowboy hat that costs $250, a cowboy shirt that costs $85, a pair of Levis so worn out you wouldn't give them to the Salvation Army, a leather, cowboy belt worth $2.50 with a $200 sterling silver bronc busting buckle, a $1000 pair of alligator hide cowboy boots. He will be wearing a $3500 diamond ring, an $8000 gold Presidential day date Rolex watch, a $3000 diamond set gold nugget hanging on a $1500 gold chain, a $100 set of gold Cross pens in his shirt pocket, a $75 pair of Carrera sunshades, and the rest of his gear is packed into a cardboard box, tied up with an old piece of rope.

The English engineers will be in three-piece suits, bowler hats, carrying their umbrellas, (brolly), and their luggage made by Gucci, in the finest Italian leather.

Then there are the divers: a worn-out pair of jeans, (not Levis) a holey T-shirt, and a worn-out pair of "tenny" shoes, wearing a stainless steel, Rolex helium purge SUBMARINER, with all the rest of his gear wadded up, and stuffed into a bright, yellow, plastic bag, with UNI-SUIT printed on the side which he stole from the last job he was on.

What I'm saying, is it takes all kinds to make the world go around, or different strokes for different folks.

A Tender To Trust

Many years ago, there was a job that required a diver and his tender to be at work every night at midnight. Back in those days, the divers were still using what we in the diving industry refer to as "heavy gear" or "standard gear," in other words: the old diving helmets we see our movie heroes wearing, like John Wayne diving into the dark, murky depths, braving all the fearful creatures that are lurking there, waiting to gobble him up.

This particular job was working on a pier doing some repair work that required no surface support, other than his diving gear and the diving tender.

Woody and his tender, Bob, had been in a bar having a few drinks before reporting for work at midnight. When they arrived at the job site, it was a cold winter night with the wind blowing and cold enough to freeze the balls off a brass monkey. They met the project engineer who gave them their instructions for the evening and said he would come out and see how they were getting on later. He was going to stay in the Port-a-cabin that was at the end of the pier, which he used as an office. Not only that, but it also had a coffee pot and a nice warm heater.

It wasn't till after 6 o'clock in the morning that the engineer finally got up enough courage to brave the cold and go down to the pier to check how the boys were getting on. As he was walking down the pier, he could see that Bob was sitting on a box, hunched up with his head buried into his chest holding Woody's hose. As he got closer, he saw that Bob was actually asleep.

Wondering what the hell was going on, he woke Bob and inquired as to how Woody was getting on. Bob mumbled something about he's doing just fine, which the engineer knew was bullshit, so the engineer walked over to the side of the pier to look for himself. And what does he see? There is Woody lying inside of a girder with his helmet propped against a pile, sound asleep. The tide had gone out leaving him high and dry six feet above the water.

The One With The Coffee Mug

Divers are notorious for doing things underwater that they were not sent down to do. One that comes to mind is of a diver named Dave who was sent down on a dive to attach a guide wire to a guidepost on a B.O.P. (Blow Out Preventer) stack.

This was in fairly shallow water (about 120'). To attach a guide wire in this depth of water is usually a 5-minute job. After about half an hour, and a number of requests from the diving supervisor for Dave to tell him how he was getting on, Dave's only reply was that, "Everything's fine." The supervisor, finally fed up with this answer, told Dave to get ready to leave bottom and he would send someone else down to complete the job. Dave then told him, "I finished the job 30 minutes ago, I'm looking for my coffee cup that I dropped over the side last week."

You may have wondered how I came up with a title for this collection of rubbish like *SHAKE ME IF IT'S SUNNY*. It wasn't my idea at all, it was another diver's idea for the title of a book he planned to write along the same lines as this one, and I stole it from him.

What you really were referring to was how did the title originate, and that is a long story that I will attempt to cut down to a short story.

Back in the heydays of the North Sea when things were really booming and the construction work was proceeding at as rapid a pace as humanly possible, every large construction company was trying to get their share of the work. These companies would keep large teams of divers on board just in case they were required. Consequentially, there were numerous occasions of days on end that the divers had no duties requiring their presence on deck. Our fearless deep sea divers during these slack periods had a tenacity to stay up most of the night playing games of chance or some other such foolishness, then sleeping most of the following day.

This practice did not sit particularly well with the rest of the crew who were working their asses off 12 hours on and 12 hours off for months at a time. But divers being the considerate, individualistic characters they are, had no qualms whatsoever of asking one of the crew members on the 0001 to 1200 shift to wake him up in the morning if the sun was shining, so he could lay on the helideck and catch a few rays, or as the divers would say,

"SHAKE ME IF IT'S SUNNY."

Divers are known for their weird sense of humor and what they think is funny, most people in this world would think of as sick.

Divers are famous for shocking people by telling them how good it feels to piss in their wet suits when they're cold and just how wonderful that hot piss feels running down their legs. Most people will respond with something along the lines about being "KINKY," to which the divers always respond, "Of course that's kinky, he's into rubber after all."

Taking The Proverbial Piss

There was one barge captain who hated divers with a purple passion; all they were to him were "necessary evils." He would go to extreme lengths to make life as miserable as possible for any divers who were on his vessel. So with his attitude, it made it impossible for the divers to please him. It became a challenge to the divers to see who could do the most evil, sly, and devious things to this Captain Bligh. It got to the point where he couldn't leave his dinner without returning to find for example that his soup had been heavily spiked with Tabasco chili sauce or some such thing or if he went to pick up his binoculars on the bridge, he could find that someone had smeared black grease on the eye pieces. One time, his shoelaces were so knotted that they had to be cut off, and even grease was put inside his boots. There would always be one sock missing when his clothes returned from the laundry, his knickers would frequently go missing, and his personal mail had a tendency to be several weeks late, especially if the letters were from his wife.

Well, the captain was fairly sure that all his misfortune was not due to lady luck alone, that it was almost certainly those fucking divers who were responsible. But, unfortunately, he could never catch them in the act. So, without proof, he just had to live with the misery they were creating for him.

But the one thing that the divers did time after time, right before his eyes, that he never did cotton on to, was to piss on his office floor. It was his practice to call a diver to his office to grill him over hot coals as soon as the diver came out of the water. These devious animals would stand in front of the captain looking humble as the captain gave them an ass chewing, pissing in their wet suits, and pretending that all the fluid gathering at their feet was just sea water draining from their suits.

The captain had the chief engineer checking the plumbing over the whole barge, trying to find where that shithouse odor was coming from that was always present in his office.

A Saltwater Soak

Another story concerning a barge captain took place in West Africa a number of years ago. This captain had contracted some sort of skin disorder and was having no luck with creams and lotions that the barge medic was prescribing, so when the divers convinced him that the best thing in the world for dermatitis was saltwater soaks, the captain decided to give it a try. I'm told that it was one of the funniest things you ever saw—the captain hanging from the crane over the side in a basket, up to his chin in the sea, balls ass naked, with his cowboy hat on to protect his bald head from getting sunburned.

But in this case, the laugh was on the fucking divers, because you see, those saltwater soaks cured the captain's dermatitis.

You have noticed that I frequently use the term 'fucking divers', that's because in the oil patch, divers are always referred to in this manner, i.e. "wake up those fucking divers; tell those fucking divers; go get them fucking divers; them fucking divers did" . . . etc., etc.

Divers are so frequently called 'fucking divers' that they even occasionally refer to themselves as 'fucking divers'. I had a diver tell me that he had been a commercial diver for five years before he realized that fucking and divers were not one word.

I overheard a barge foreman tell a diving supervisor that one of his fucking divers had lied, to which the supervisor replied, "That diver may piss on your foot and tell you that it is raining but he wouldn't lie to you."

Here are a couple of quick diving jokes for you to tell at your local tonight.

Q. How do you sink an Irish submarine.
A. Send down a diver and have him knock on the hatch.

Q. How do you circumcise a whale.
A. Send fore-a-SKIN diver.

Q. How can you tell when a diver is lying.
A. When his lips are moving.

"But It Fits Together Perfectly."

I had a diving supervisor tell me this story about a young diver that he had working for him a few years back on a tie-in job. (A tie-in is a pipeline job where you use what we call a spool-piece to connect two ends of a pipeline together or one end of a pipeline to a riser which runs up the leg of an offshore structure.

This is usually accomplished by either a hyperbaric weld or more likely with some means of a mechanical connector, or as in this particular case, with bolted flanges and a gasket [referred to as an AX or RX ring type gasket].)

This young diver was sent down to align the two flanges, install the ring gasket, and begin to put the bolts into the flanges.

The diving supervisor told me that he figured that there was something amiss when this young gent seemed to be making much better progress than even a highly experienced diver would be expected to accomplish. They were diving in very shallow water so he instructed one of the other divers to throw on a set of tanks and nip down to the bottom and see what our young hero was up to as there was no way in hell he could have aligned the flanges, installed the ring gasket, and put in the bolts, considering the time he had been down. So, the diver hit the water and within a couple of minutes was back on the surface telling the supervisor, "You better get that diver (sic) off the bottom because we have another one of these guys that doesn't know his ass from a hole in the ground." (I think you know what that means by now) "That cunt is down there putting the bolts in the flanges but the problem is that the ring gasket is still laying on top of the pipeline."

So, when our irate supervisor got this "cunt" back to the surface and asked him what the hell he thought he was doing putting the bolts in without first installing the ring, our budding hero replies, "The pipeline and spool-piece fitted together perfectly, and I didn't need that spacer."

It takes all kinds of folks to make the world go around, and I guess even stupidity has its place.

Think Before You Act

We were putting a small structure on bottom one day in 200 feet of water that required the use of ballast tanks to assist with the lowering operation.

Fred, one of the best divers I ever met in my life, was on bottom opening the ballast tanks valves which were two-inch, quarter swing valves, which are like a guillotine on the inside in that the ball closes off the bore of the valve. While Fred was de-rigging the lifting gear, he made a mistake and got too close to one of these valves that he had already opened, and the suction of almost 100 PSI of hydrostatic head sucked two of Fred's fingers into the valve. Fred was unable to pull his fingers out due to force of the suction. When it was suggested to Fred that he may be able to close the valve and get his finger out, he replied, "Yes, and probably leave the tips of my fingers in the valve." He was told not to do anything and that the stand-by diver was on his way down and would open the valve on the other end, which would relieve the suction pressure. This was accomplished and Fred came away with nothing hurt but his professional pride, but with a healthy respect for open flood valves underwater.

I wish I could say that that was the end of this little episode, but unfortunately it's not. The very next day, two men, one a roughneck, the other a roustabout working on the platform near where we were anchored, were discussing the incident of the diver who was trapped on bottom the day before. The roughneck was explaining to the roustabout what had happened (at this time they were examining a valve that was identical to the one Fred had his fingers sucked into). As he demonstrated how the diver's fingers were stuck in the valve and explained how the stand-by diver had had to be sent down to open another valve so that the diver could get his fingers out. The roustabout asked, as he reached over closing the valve, "why didn't he just close the valve like this?" This severed two of the roughneck's fingers.

This story just goes to show you that in the offshore oil industry, danger lurks around every corner and you don't know where it's coming from next.

Since divers live with danger at all times, it stands to reason that they approach life with a different point of view than most other people; maybe, it's something along the lines of, ". . . enjoy life while you can." I feel this is what gives them their sense of humor, a little abstract though it might be, while offshore takes the form of playing pranks on their fellow diving buddies.

Government Intervention

Since diving is a dangerous business, the various government regulatory bodies around the world, such as the U.K. Department of Energy (DOE), Norwegian Petroleum Directorate (NPD), Department of Transport (DOT), and others are constantly issuing regulations and safety recommendations to try to improve the safety standards for divers. Most of these regulations are good and really do help to improve safety, but occasionally a real 'dilly' comes along that that is just out of this world. One of the regulations that came out a couple of years back was that all hyperbaric lifeboats were to be tested with divers inside to determine that the divers' internal core temperature didn't rise above a safe level.

In order to do this, a core temperature thermometer was arranged and sent offshore for the diving crew to comply with the safety requirements as stipulated by this new regulation. As this could be considered as a bit off the beaten path of what is expected of divers, it was decided that one of the old divers who had come ashore and taken an office job would accompany this instrument.

He was to explain this new regulation to the diving crew and why it was necessary to have a temperature probe stuck up someone's ass, in order to get a core temperature reading to satisfy the government Inspector.

And also, as we were one man short of the fifteen men required to get a full test load certificate, he would be the fifteenth man.

He arrived on board and got the temperature test probe wired up inside the chamber so that the results could be read and recorded outside the chamber while they were under pressure on the inside.

Finally, all the preparations were completed and the time had arrived to put the test subjects under pressure. Would you believe that not one of those 'deep sea divers' would volunteer to be the test subject—to have this probe stuck up his rectum. It was suggested by the other divers that since our old diver was the senior man on board with the most experience, someone who all these 'superhero divers' had been looking up to for years, he should be the one to show them the way. To which he replied something to the effect of "Fuck you guys." Then they asked if he wouldn't do it, would he agree to drawing names out of a hat? To which he agreed, but only if he was the one who did the draw, as he didn't trust the rest of those assholes to do it fairly.

The draw was arranged and all fifteen names, including our old diver's, were written on little pieces of paper; these were carefully folded and placed in a hat for our (fearless?) hero to draw from. The big moment had arrived, he carefully reached into the hat and withdrew a little square of paper, unfolded it to announce the unfortunate loser, and in a state of shock, read out his own name. He instantly started bitching about lady luck and that he had been a gambler all his life and would have bet a month's pay on fifteen to one odds.

The crew entered the chamber and for the next eight hours took great delight in watching and making rude comments as every fifteen minutes, the internal core temperature probe was carefully greased with boy butter and shoved up our hero's ass. Everyone enjoying all that swearing and cursing at lady luck, what a rotten no-good bitch she was, and he was never coming offshore again, so on and on it went for eight hours.

When the test was finally completed, and our hero exited the chamber, he found half of the barge crew there to greet him all with huge shit-eating grins. This was the first moment that the dawning light of realization hit him. He had been had. He listened, sick at heart, how the divers had substituted their names in the hat, as they distracted his attention for a moment just prior to the draw, and with fifteen neat, little, square pieces of paper with his name on all of them!

Keep An Eye On That Would You?

There was a young diver, at least he was young when this story took place, who had a glass eye (no this is not the story about old wooden eye). Seems, he had a bit of a sense of humor regarding his glass eye and just loved springing the fact on unsuspecting folk at the most inappropriate times so as to get the most shock value for his little pranks. The one that stands out in my mind is the one that took place on a drill ship off Italy. He had arrived a day or two before, and as this was his first trip on board, he was just getting to know the diving crew, when as always happens when you least expect it, the supervisor was told by the tool pusher that he needed them to make a dive for some reason or other. Well, the supervisor felt that he should make a dive with this new hand to check him out in the bell, and just see in general what kind of diver his new man was (it might also have had something to do with the fact that we received depth pay in those days, and the supervisor was saving up to buy himself a new wopmobile).

The supervisor briefed our lad on all the details of the job, went through all the systems inside the bell so our lad would know what to do as he would be the bell tender. The supervisor planned to make the lock out himself, as he wanted to make sure the job got done, and he didn't, as of yet, know if our lad could even swim.

Finally, it was dive time. Everybody was in their position and ready to go. The bell was lowered through the moon pool and was on its way to the bottom. The diving supervisor was going over last-minute details and emergency procedures with the new hand who was all ears. It was obvious to the supervisor that this lad was keen and eager to learn and there was no doubt that he meant to please.

In due course, they arrived on bottom and the supervisor donned his equipment in preparation for blow-down (This is the moment in all bounce dive modes when the tension is at its highest—sort of like first-night jitters, butterflies in the stomach, just prior to opening the blow down valve and compressing to 400 feet at 100 feet a minute on a gas mixture of oxygen, helium, and quite often nitrogen. There will be a temperature change of many degrees on a 500-foot blowdown. I've seen the temperature go from 60F to 110F. That is a 50 degree increase in 5 minutes and I can tell you it will knock the snot out of you). Also, during these rapid compression rates there is another factor that affects you a great deal, the medical term is High Pressure Nervous Syndrome, to a diver it is known as the shakes or trembles. On some dives, you get the shakes so bad that by the time you hit the bottom, you can't hit your ass with both hands. Also, you are very concerned that you will not be able to equalize the pressure in your inner ear. If you can't at these compression rates, it is only a matter of seconds before you rupture your ear drums, so as you can see, all these factors have a bearing on the nervousness and apprehension just prior to blowdown.

Well, to continue, the supervisor was watching our lad closely to see how he was handling himself, and the lad was showing no adverse effects. The supervisor took off his Oyster Perpetual, gold, Rolex diving watch and laid it on top of the carbon dioxide scrubber and told our lad to look after it for him. Our lad replied, "Don't worry I will keep an EYE on it for you" and popped out his glass eye and placed it on top of the watch!

The supervisor later remarked he didn't know whether to shit or go blind (bad pun) but knew for a fact that he had found himself a diver.

That makes for a fair, little story, but the next day the supervisor called in to give his weekly report and got the big boss. He mentioned in passing that the operation manager had sent him a one-eyed diver.

Hearing this, the big boss decided to have a little fun with his ops manager, so he called him on the phone and began giving him an 'ass chewing' about sending out one-eyed divers (just to stir him up a little). But our friend, the operations manager, who was quick witted and even quicker of tongue replied, "Hell, that's alright, just tell the supervisor not to use him on observation dives."

The Man From Atlantis

Divers are CRAZY!! The difference between a fairy tale and a sea story is—fairy tales start *Once upon a time,* a sea story starts, "This is no shit"—the following story is not a fairy tale.

THIS IS NO SHIT! This sort of stunt could be pulled in the Mediterranean Sea, where the water is warm, but no diver is crazy enough to pull this stunt in the North Sea where the water is so cold it gets to those brass monkey danglers every time.

This crazy diver was the bell tender on a saturation job and had been sitting in the bell for almost four hours, bitching about how bored he was and how he wanted something to do. The surface crew kept telling him to shut up; they were busy trying to do a job and didn't have time to listen to his bitching.

They were diving in 400 feet of water and had an ROV on the job assisting the lock out diver (an ROV is a Remote Operated Vehicle, which in most cases, is nothing more than a flying eyeball). The top side crew were watching the TV monitor to see what the diver was doing, when what should appear in front of the TV camera? Would you believe! One balls ass naked bell tender free diving in his birthday suit! He swam gracefully up to the TV camera, turned around, using both of his hands to spread the cheeks of his ass, shot them a big brown eye, gave them a royal wave, and then swam slowly back to the bell.

I won't even go into what the diving superintendent may or may not have said but I did hear him muttering something about that goddamn idiot thinks he's the 'man from Atlantis.' It may have been crazy; it was more likely stupid but I still think it was funny as hell.

Sweet Thing And The Animal

When the diver reads this, I may receive a letter bomb in the post from him as this story took place over fifteen years ago, and he has just about lived this humiliation down—so he thinks!! Anyway, the point is, he is not going to be exactly overjoyed to have this subject reopened.

I wasn't there, so I may not get all the gory details just right, but I hope to portray this tale in such a manner that all the men concerned will recognize themselves, without letting the whole world know their identity. Why I should worry about a slur on their character is beyond me.

As I said, this story took place over fifteen years ago on a drilling rig in the North Sea. This crew of divers had one man in the team who can only be described as an animal, and another diver who can only be described as a very sweet, nice guy, always very kind and polite. What the hell he was doing being a diver with that type of character, I surely will never know. His character made him a perfect target for abuse from our animal friend, who took great delight in keeping 'Sweet Thing' stirred up.

There was a constant stream of requests thrown at him from the animal suggesting that it would be nice if 'Sweet Thing' would submit to an act of buggery. Sweet Thing always headed off these suggestions in some form or fashion, but not without some degree of embarrassment.

As Lady Luck would have it, it turned out that these two wound up as bell partners for a dive one day.

The dive went off without a hitch and both divers were in good spirts as they had had a very successful dive. When they arrived back on the surface and the bell was locked onto the surface deck decompression chamber (DDC), and while they transferred into the main lock, the animal started trying to convince 'Sweet Thing' that now they had the perfect opportunity to participate in some fun and games along the lines suggested above. As they were going to be undergoing decompression for many hours to come, it would give them something pleasurable to do.

In the meantime, the rest of the crew settled down for a long decompression watch in the deck control van (DCV) and were listening on the radio to these erotic suggestions that the animal was badgering 'Sweet Thing' with.

This badgering kept up for several hours, with 'Sweet Thing' becoming more and more frustrated. No matter what he said, the animal carried on relentlessly with the suggestions that 'Sweet Thing' would really enjoy having an erect tool stuck up his posterior end, if only he would try it. The crew outside were by this time in stitches listening to poor 'Sweet Thing' try everything in his power to get the animal to leave him alone, all to no avail.

For, if there was one thing the animal was, he was persistent.

By this time, the animal had gotten his proudest possession out and was chasing SWEET THING around the chamber saying, "Come on, 'Sweet Thing,' let me hit you in the shitter," with 'Sweet Thing' shouting back, "NO." The animal, replies, "try it, you'll like it." 'Sweet Thing', who was by now near to tears, in a total state of desperate frustration, shouted back to the animal, as the crew outside listen in with glee, "I've tried it and I don' t like it."

Now, you too know why I will not be overly surprised when that letter bomb arrives in the mail. But I don't think that will really be anything to worry about, as it will most likely only go poof.

Wicked Wanda And The Royal Navy

A number of years ago, I think 1979, if my faulty memory serves me correctly, there was a small article that appeared in all the daily tabloids on about page 10 so you can see just how important this event was to the daily lives of all Her Britannic Majesty's subjects. The article was along the line of HMS something or other was mobilized from Portsmouth Harbor yesterday to pick up a body reported by a fisherman to be floating offshore etc. Now I can tell the actual story of how that body came to be floating offshore in the first place. You see the body that the Royal Navy was called to rescue was no other than Wicked Wanda, that voluptuous beauty of the sex shops; Wicked Wanda, the blow-up doll with more orifices for sticking organic matter into than your mother's vegetable strainer.

One of the divers working on a job in the middle of the North Sea just could not face the thought of leaving that wonderful city of sin, Amsterdam, without female companionship. So, in a moment of drunken desire on his last night's run ashore, his passion overcame his sense of self-preservation. He parted with a pocketful of hard-earned pesos, that he had converted to goffers (that's guilders like in Dutch to you misinformed unfortunates), and purchased Wicked Wanda, the girl of his (wet) dreams.

Our hero, feeling very proud of himself, duly smuggled Wicked Wanda on board the vessel and into his cabin, where he promptly inflated Wanda, by blowing into her oral inflation tube (I wonder if you could interpret that as a blow job). He tucked her up with tender loving care into his bunk, crawled into the sack with her, placed his arms around her, and promised never ending passion for her, and instantly passed out, totally oblivious to all that took place around him for the next 12 hours.

The rest of his diving mates arrived at all hours of the night and enjoyed enormously the sight of 'El Drunko' snuggling into his lady love's arms.

The next day, the captain started a search for the stowaway that he overheard the divers whispering about at breakfast. Some broad named Wanda that one of the divers had in his cabin. Well, the diving superintendent clued the captain in on what was going on, he had a great relieved laugh, and said something about "Hoping 'El Drunko' had enjoyed himself" and went about his business. But now the cat was out of the bag, and divers being divers wanted in on the action so 'El Drunko' was shit out of luck. The diving crew adopted Wicked Wanda as one of their own; she became the most popular person on board, she was sought by all the divers, they all wanted the privilege to be the one to escort Wanda to dinner, where she had her own special place at the divers table. She was queen, with all the divers paying her the most wonderful compliments, and all of them vying for her charms.

Wanda was so much in demand for the nightly movie, that the divers had to draw up a rota so that everyone got a fair chance to delight in her charms. The lucky man of the evening would take Wanda to the cinema, usually escorted by a large crowd of envious males. Wanda would get the best seat in the house, where she would sit with her arm around her escort's shoulder, enjoying the movie.

Alas, Wicked Wanda was beginning to show the strain of all the attention from this 30-man strong team of rough, tough, North Sea divers. All this night and day partying was starting to show on poor Wanda; her once peaches and cream complexion was looking decidedly blemished. Her long, midnight, black hair was in need of attention; the bright gleam that had been in her dark eyes was starting to fade. Being the only female in this all-male crew was taking its toll. Poor Wicked Wanda was growing old, she was aging before the divers very eyes. You could hear the whispers starting behind Wanda's back: ". . . old before her time, burned out, worn out, losing her charms, washed-up, etc." The strain finally become too much for Wicked Wanda—her health was failing. The men had performed a number of emergency operations on her weakened air vessels to try to save her, but this was all to no avail, for in her worn-out state, she finally ruptured a major air vessel and expired. This sad day was the very day that the diving job was completed, and all of Wanda's many admirers were to depart to the beach.

The diving crew felt that it was only right that they should give a decent ceremony to one who had given them so much pleasure. They gave Wanda a final bath, repaired her rupture so she could once more be inflated with pride, dressed her in her most fetching garments—a black cupless bra and matching crotchless knickers.

With great sadness and sorrow, Wicked Wanda's remains were committed to the depths, as man has traditionally been doing since the first crew of sailors set out to sail the oceans of our wonderful world.

So, now you know why the Royal Navy was called out on that day many years ago. And even though this is a sad story, it has a happy ending because you see, Wicked Wanda didn't go to that place some people refer to as the happy hunting grounds in the sky. She was picked up by a bunch of horny Royal Navy matelots, and where would Wicked Wanda be happier. Surely that must be heaven for a rubber doll, even a rubber doll well past her prime.

On a serious note: there was in actual fact a very serious incident offshore a few years ago involving a rubber doll and a couple of Arabs. It seems one of the Arabs found the other one making love to his rubber doll; this upset him to the point that he pulled a knife and stabbed the man. And here I was thinking all this time that the Arabs were into goats, sheep, camels and pretty boys. I overheard an Arab say one day that he would rather hear a fat boy fart, than a pretty girl sing.

Here is another "Quickie" for you to tell at the pub tonight.

Why do you call a camel the ship of the desert? Because it's filled with ARAB SEMEN.

Cookie Went To War

A project engineer was telling me of the time he was working offshore as a field engineer for a large construction company. Before I go any further, I should tell you what a field engineer is:

A field engineer is the lowest, slowest, dumbest concentration of organic matter in the known universe making up a body known as Homo sapiens—a human. On an offshore project, he rates one half on a 1 to 10 stroke/power/pull scale. On such a scale, a trainee diver rates one, the barge captain ranks very high indeed, as much as 9, depending on his skills and attitude. The only man offshore who will ever rate 10 is the chief cook because if he ever wobbles (an offshore term designating that a man is refusing to work for some reason real or imagined) the whole crew does not work as men offshore, just like the army who marches on its bellies, the offshore hands work on their bellies; so needless to say, the chief cook has a tremendous amount of stroke/power/pull.

As this engineer was telling me, it seems that the chief cook had thrown a wobble because someone had sworn at him in the mess hall and he didn't know who it was, and he was refusing to prepare any chow until he got an apology from the guilty man. As I have pointed out, somewhere in this collection of rubbish, when an oil company is paying many thousands of dollars a day for equipment and crews to do a job, they expect production and if a barge is not working, it sure as hell is not producing, so this puts a great deal of pressure on the barge captain to keep the crew happy so that there are no hang ups and the job progresses smoothly.

So here we have a problem. The cook won't cook, and the crew will not come clean and confess who cursed at the cook, and the client is getting upset and threating to run the barge off the project unless this dilemma is resolved with dispatch.

The barge captain finally decides that the only way he is going to get this problem resolved is to get the whole crew together in the mess hall, face to face with the cook where he is sure that someone will confess and he can get the barge back onto the payroll.

As the crew files into the mess hall, the various departments, i.e., the deck crew, the riggers, the below decks crew, the divers all sit down in separate groups. This is nothing unusual—these people congregate together as they work together.

So, here he has the crew together, with the chief cook and himself standing in front of the men, he explains that they have a problem with the client, and the only thing required to solve this whole dilemma is that someone admits that he swore at the chief cook and apologize, so that the whole problem can be resolved.

Well, needless to say no one will confess and the meeting is getting nowhere. Finally, one of the barge foremen says to the captain, "Hell, nobody is going to confess, we don't even know what he's been called" to which the barge captain thought for a moment and then having made his decision, replied, "All I wanted to know is, WHO CALLED THE COOK A CUNT?" There was deathly silence for a few moments, and then from the section where the divers were sitting, there was a voice heard to say, "WHO CALLED THAT CUNT A COOK?"

No Hands

It goes without saying that offshore a large portion of the men's conversation has a tendency to deal with the females of our species. That is because these men spend so much of their time in male companionship, it only stands to reason that this exciting topic of conversation is uppermost in their minds.

As you might imagine, this conversation often deals with the sexual aspects of the female gender, and what they are going to do with the lady love of their life when they hit the beach, and so on.

One day after a hard day of diving, the divers were sitting around looking at some of the sexy literature that abounds offshore, when one of the divers, while looking at a rather fetching piece in one of the higher class glossy publications, made the comment that the sex machine that he was looking at would probably cause him to have a wet dream that night, to which one of the other divers replied, "that is, if you don't wake up in time to help it out yourself," which caused a few chuckles from his mates.

Ian, one of the divers, didn't laugh. He just sat there looking perplexed when it was noticed that be seemed a bit puzzled, he was asked what was bothering him. He replied that, "I have been listening all these years to stories about you guys having wet dreams, but I have never had one."

After his mates had gotten over the shock of hearing this confession, and after quite a lengthy conversation and discussion on why he had never experienced this sensation, it was suggested that if he left his proudest possession alone for a few nights, that he may experience this most pleasurable discharge sensation for himself. Ian agreed to abstain from his nightly activities to determine if this had anything to do with his having never experienced a spontaneous ejaculation.

Though everyone had enjoyed a good laugh at Ian's expense, nothing more was thought about this particular evening's conversation, until a few mornings later when the divers were awakened by a loud commotion in the main passageway. As they came tumbling out of their cabins, thinking the barge must be on fire or sinking, they found the cause of the uproar and confusion to be none other than Ian.

Ian was in his birthday suit, running up and down the corridor, balls ass naked, carrying the sheet off his bed pointing to a large wet, gooey stain in the middle and shouting, "look guys look, no hands."

So, there you have it, after only twenty-nine years, nine months, and nine days, Ian, the deep sea diver extraordinaire, had experienced his first, hands off, unassisted, offshore climax. I have heard of hands-on experience, but I must admit that this is the first time I have ever heard of hands-off experience.

CHAPTER
FIVE

Near Misses

Not all things that happen to divers are funny or full of humor, some things are very serious indeed. There are numerous near misses and close escapes, and even sometimes, death involved. I will not approach death in this book, because this book is meant to be fun and there is nothing funny about death. We who have been in the diving game for any length of time have lost too many good friends to accidents, and not all of them were diving accidents, to feel anything but great sorrow when we remember our unfortunate fellow divers who are no longer with us.

Most of the things you will read in this chapter will be in a serious frame, but even serious matters usually have some humor that comes to light after the event.

Anyone that has ever been to sea, learns to respect the powers and forces the sea has at its disposal. If you don't learn that respect, and quickly, you're not going to be around very long.

The North Sea has many moods, and they are all unpredictable, many say like a woman, some even say like their wives. A subject that I wouldn't know anything about. I have seen the North Sea as smooth as a mill pond, only to have a storm force 10, blowing fifty or sixty knots two hours later, with waves building up to 35 or 40 feet. Green water washing everything on deck into the sea that hasn't been properly secured, and white water bursting over the bridge. Vessels of all sizes and configurations rolling, pitching, and heaving so violently that it was almost impossible to remain standing. The old saying, "One hand for the ship and one hand for yourself," must have originated in conditions such as these.

The above-described conditions are not the worst, they are the kind you expect to have many times each year; they become a common occurrence that you just learn to live with, knowing that if you have a few days of weather downtime, it's time to catch up on your reading or sleep, and you may even be lucky enough to get a run ashore for a couple of nights, if the vessel's skipper decides to run for shelter.

But in your mind while you are offshore, there is always the thought that the big one, the one the experts call the 'hundred-year storm' is lurking, waiting to come charging down from its birthplace in the frozen wastes of the Far North. When it comes in the North Sea, it comes out of the Northeast, creating fear for anyone in its path, and leaving havoc in its wake; it provides a golden opportunity for the religious man to speak to his god.

It's named the Hundred-Year Storm, because these storms are only supposed to occur every 100 years. I have been in two 100-year storms in less than twenty years. All the 'Old North Sea Hands' will remember them, the years 1967 and 1973—if my memory serves me correctly, if not, look it up for yourselves. These monsters can't be described, you must experience them to understand what the sea is capable of, the sheer unbelievable power and force of the combined winds and waves is enough to bring fear into the heart of a marble statue, not to mention, the heart of a 'baby diver', like myself in 1967.

I can assure you, that the figure "100" occurs in several ways in the Hundred Year Storm i.e., 100-foot waves and 100-knot winds. If you see one of those mountainous monsters coming at you and it doesn't put the fear of God into you, you're a much braver man than me. And I don't even believe in a god (But that's a different subject).

When this storm took place, the drilling rig we were on was one of the largest and finest built at that time, one of the very first Semi-Submersibles to come into the North Sea. The crew felt very safe and confident that nothing could happen that would give cause for worry. As a matter of fact, we were all treating this storm like a spectacular show for the first hour or so, but the heart of the storm had not really arrived then. We were on deck with our cameras recording this event, so we could impress our lady friends when we got ashore with documented facts of what brave and wonderful men we were. Then the real fury of the storm arrived and we had to face the awful truth that maybe we were not quite as brave as we had always believed ourselves to be.

During the build-up of the storm, the crew had discovered that one of the flotation pontoons was taking in water and that the pumps were just barely able to keep up with the ingress of sea water. As the storm increased, the cause of the leak was found to be a crack in a subsea weld on the pontoon. It was further determined that the crack must be propagating and that the ballast pumps were now no longer capable of keeping up with the inflow of sea water. In short, we were slowly sinking, and no one could possibly tell what state the subsea crack was in. There was a very possible chance that it would totally fail at any time and, needless to say, there were some very worried men on board that drilling rig.

The decision was taken to evacuate the crew to safety. There was absolutely no possibility that the crew could take to the lifeboats and no chance, even if there had been a vessel, for the men to transfer to another vessel in those mountainous waves and seas.

The heroes, and I mean REAL HEROES, of this story are the Norwegian helicopter pilots that volunteered to fly a Sikorski S-61 helicopter in hurricane force winds, blowing in excess of 90 knots, to rescue us.

What a tremendous job they did, flying from Stavanger to the rig's location several times to rescue the whole crew and what skills these men had to land and take off from a heaving, pitching vessel in a storm of such magnitude. It was an experience of a lifetime to just be a passenger. Sitting in that helicopter, watching him "FEEL" the wind and deck under his aircraft, and to see the skill to lift a fully loaded chopper into 90+ knots of wind, to see and feel a helicopter almost flying on its side, when the wind caught it, for what seemed at the time, like forever.

I heard that they had to replace all the seats in that chopper because they all were ruined—large holes in the center of the cushions where our assholes had been chewing, and even some of them had smelly, brown stains.

As it turned out, the drilling rig survived the storm, but required extensive repairs in a dockyard. Over 300 tons of steel was added to reinforce it and replace the various things that were damaged or lost.

That's when you appreciate the power those waves generate, when you see handrails, ladders, etc. ripped loose and lost over the side, steel torn as if it were tissue paper. This story had a happy ending, mainly due to some very brave men and a lot of luck, and I guess the moral of this story is NEVER, I say NEVER, underestimate the sea, because if you do, it will surely jump up and bite you on the ass.

In 1973, I was working on another drilling vessel, a ship-shaped vessel called a drill ship. We had just arrived from West Africa where the weather was warm and sunny, the normal everyday dress was a pair of cut-off jeans and shower shoes. Then to find ourselves in the middle of the North Sea in December up to our asses in snow was enough to make us want to cry.

The 100-Year Storm

We had just arrived and finished setting up on location, all anchors ran and holding. This particular location was an old site that they had abandoned some eighteen months before when a bad storm had come through and blown the drill ship off location just as they were in the process of picking up the Blow Out Preventer (BOP) off the bottom. Unfortunately, they weren't able to finish retrieving the BOP and it had fallen to the bottom.

So, the first priority was to recover the abandoned BOP. You must keep in mind that in the early Seventies there was very little commercial saturation diving being done, so most jobs were done by bell bounce diving, where the bell is only a means of transporting the divers to and from the bottom. In this form of diving, the divers must spend relatively long periods of time decompressing for very short bottom times. The location we were on was in about

450 feet of water and if my memory serves me correctly, it required about 18 hours of decompression for only 40 minutes of bottom time which reminds me how well we used to plan dives in order to achieve maximum production in the short time a diver had on bottom. (Some of the divers who read this book will know what I'm talking about. In these modern days of high technology with multimillion dollars of saturation equipment, it takes more than 40 minutes to get some of the divers out of the bell and on the job). I digress again but that is a story I will tell before I finish this book, otherwise I personally will not feel that it's finished.

After a couple of dives, we had the BOP rigged and almost ready to lift. It required just one more dive to complete the job. The weather report at this time was not very good, but we knew there was enough time to complete the dive, and then the crew could recover the BOP, and we could complete our decompression on the way into harbor. As any diver can tell you, a 5-minute job can take hours, or a long job can take minutes, it all depends, if Murphy wants to take a hand. Well, Murphy left the divers alone this time, but decided to help out the vessels crew. The dive went as planned, but the divers were on full bottom time, so requiring a hell of a long stay in the decompression chamber which was located on the main deck and being only about 12 feet above the water.

As I said, Murphy decided to take a hand and instead of an hour or so for the crew to get the BOP to the surface and secured on deck, it took several hours, by which time the weather had picked up to the point that the anchor handling vessel couldn't pick up the drill ship's anchors. So now, instead of sailing into a nice quiet harbor and riding out a storm that had been forecasted to be rough, we found ourselves in the middle of the North Sea preparing to ride out a storm on anchors.

At this point, I must point out to those of you who aren't in the know, that the last thing any captain working in the oil patch will do is cut his anchor chains. You can bet your ass that when he does, it is to save lives or his ship. When you understand how much one of these vessels' costs, each and everyday, and that it only gets paid when it's actually working, it's a cardinal sin to cut the chains, because it will require a week or more to recover all the anchors, during which time the vessel is still costing all that cash and not making a penny. Not to mention the damage it would do to the vessel's reputation, and you would not believe just how important a vessel's reputation is when it comes to being hired for that all important next job.

The storm that is forecasted as a force 10 on the Beaufort scale, with winds 48 to 55 knots, reaches force 10 and continues into force eleven, steadily increasing to force 12 where the scale stops, and is described as a hurricane. Winds 64 knots and over, Beaufort does not predict, as the height of the waves and seas vary according to location, water depth, currents, duration of storm, etc., but I can tell you, in the North Sea when you are in a Force 12, you can expect waves anywhere from 40 feet up to 60 feet.

So here we were early in the evening, on anchors, in a force 12 hurricane with two divers in a decompression chamber 12 feet above the normal sea level and we were anticipating at least 12 hours before we could even think about getting them out of that pot. The one thing that was working in our favor was Murphy didn't interfere with the direction the seas were coming. They were coming straight into the stern of the drill ship, and the ship was riding as well as could be expected. (If we had been unlucky and the seas had hit us from any direction other than dead ahead or dead astern, we would have been in a world of trouble, and we may have still been out there feeding the fish and crabs).

By the time the crew realized that this wasn't a normal run of the mill storm force 10, and that we just may be in for a rough ride, it was too late to do anything about the anchor chains. You must keep in mind, that this was in 1973, on an older drill ship. Not like today, with computers and remote controls to do everything except flush the shitter for you. On this vessel, if you wanted to pay out or pull in on an anchor, you had to do it from the anchor winch, and by this time it was impossible for any man to be on deck except, of course, my two divers undergoing decompression in the chamber on deck. Here they were at a pressure equivalent to 300+ feet of sea water with 15 to 20 feet of green water over the top of that chamber a good percentage of the time. My asshole was so tight you couldn't drive a nail up it with a 16 lb. sledgehammer. While you are thinking about that, what state do you think those two divers were in? They never did tell me what they really thought, but my guess is that they had already bent over and placed their heads between their legs and kissed their asses goodbye.

The other fortunate thing was the equipment foreman and his crew had had the foresight to install the dive control console above the main deck, otherwise we wouldn't have been able to maintain life support to the divers. Being located where it was, it was well-protected from any chance of a large wave flooding it, and also, the dive watch crew could be changed out by carefully crossing the drill pipe rack, which had been strung with lifelines.

Force 12, early evening, and the winds and waves were still increasing. I am praying to King Neptune not to screw those two divers and hoping like hell that the welder who had welded down the decompression chamber was thinking about welding, and not about how hot his rod was.

And, Oh please, don't let any of the critical piping, hose whips, wiring and other critical equipment necessary to keep those two

STANDARD AIR DECOMPRESSION TABLE

Depth (feet)	Bottom time (min)	Time first stop (min:sec)	50	40	30	20	10	Total ascent (min:sec)	Repetitive group
40	200						0	0:40	*
	210	0:30					2	2:40	N
	230	0:30					7	7:40	N
	250	0:30					11	11:40	O
	270	0:30					15	15:40	O
	300	0:30					19	19:40	Z
	360	0:30					23	23:40	**
	480	0:30					41	41:40	
	720	0:30					69	69:40	
50	100						0	0:50	*
	110	0:40					3	3:50	L
	120	0:40					5	5:50	M
	140	0:40					10	10:50	M
	160	0:40					21	21:50	N
	180	0:40					29	29:50	O
	200	0:40					35	35:50	O
	220	0:40					40	40:50	Z
	240	0:40					47	47:50	Z
60	60						0	1:00	*
	70	0:50					2	3:00	K
	80	0:50					7	8:00	L
	100	0:50					14	15:00	M
	120	0:50					26	27:00	N
	140	0:50					39	40:00	O
	160	0:50					48	49:00	Z
	180	0:50					56	57:00	Z
	200	0:40				1	69	71:00	Z
	240	0:40				2	79	82:00	
	360	0:40				20	119	140:00	
	480	0:40				44	148	193:00	
	720	0:40				78	187	266:00	
70	50						0	1:10	*
	60	1:00					8	9:10	K
	70	1:00					14	15:10	L
	80	1:00					18	19:10	M
	90	1:00					23	24:10	N
	100	1:00					33	34:10	N
	110	0:50				2	41	44:10	O
	120	0:50				4	47	52:10	O
	130	0:50				6	52	59:10	O
	140	0:50				8	56	65:10	Z
	150	0:50				9	61	71:10	Z
	160	0:50				13	72	86:10	Z
	170	0:50				19	79	99:10	Z

* See No Decompression Table for repetitive groups
**Repetitive dives may not follow exceptional exposure dives

AIR DECOMPRESSION   7-9

Extracted from the US Navy Diving Manual, shows the decompression time and depths to avoid the bends.

STANDARD AIR DECOMPRESSION TABLE

Depth (feet)	Bottom time (min)	Time first stop (min:sec)	50	40	30	20	10	Total ascent (min:sec)	Repetitive group
80	40						0	1:20	*
	50	1:10					10	11:20	K
	60	1:10					17	18:20	L
	70	1:10					23	24:20	M
	80	1:00				2	31	34:20	N
	90	1:00				7	39	47:20	N
	100	1:00				11	46	58:20	O
	110	1:00				13	53	67:20	O
	120	1:00				17	56	74:20	Z
	130	1:00				19	63	83:20	Z
	140	1:00				26	69	96:20	Z
	150	1:00				32	77	110:20	Z
	180	1:00				35	85	121:20	
	240	0:50			6	52	120	179:20	
	360	0:50			29	90	160	280:20	
	480	0:50			59	107	187	354:20	
	720	0:40		17	108	142	187	455:20	
90	30						0	1:30	*
	40	1:20					7	8:30	J
	50	1:20					18	19:30	L
	60	1:20					25	26:30	M
	70	1:10				7	30	38:30	N
	80	1:10				13	40	54:30	N
	90	1:10				18	48	67:30	O
	100	1:10				21	54	76:30	Z
	110	1:10				24	61	86:30	Z
	120	1:10				32	68	101:30	Z
	130	1:00			5	36	74	116:30	Z
100	25						0	1:40	I
	30	1:30					3	4:40	*
	40	1:30					15	16:40	K
	50	1:20				2	24	27:40	L
	60	1:20				9	28	38:40	N
	70	1:20				17	39	57:40	O
	80	1:20				23	48	72:40	O
	90	1:10			3	23	57	84:40	Z
	100	1:10			7	23	66	97:40	Z
	110	1:10			10	34	72	117:40	Z
	120	1:10			12	41	78	132:40	Z
	180	1:00		1	29	53	118	202:40	
	240	1:00		14	42	84	142	283:40	
	360	0:50	2	42	73	111	187	416:40	
	480	0:50	21	61	91	142	187	503:40	
	720	0:50	55	106	122	142	187	613:40	
110	20						0	1:50	*
	25	1:40					3	4:50	H
	30	1:40					7	8:50	J
	40	1:30				2	21	24:50	L
	50	1:30				8	26	35:50	M
	60	1:30				18	36	55:50	N
	70	1:20			1	23	48	73:50	O
	80	1:20			7	23	57	88:50	Z
	90	1:20			12	30	64	107:50	Z
	100	1:20			15	37	72	125:50	Z

* See No Decompression Table for repetitive groups
**Repetitive dives may not follow exceptional exposure dives

DIVING MANUAL

Extracted from the US Navy Diving Manual, shows the decompression time and depths to avoid the bends.

guys alive, be carried away in one of those giant waves breaking over the deck chamber.

It was one of the longest nights I have ever spent in my life, and I hope like hell there will never be another one like it.

Just after midnight, the seas had increased to 70 and even 80 feet, the wind was howling and screaming like a band of demons, gusting to 90 knots on the wind gauge. The drill ship was heaving up and down straining at her anchors, and every giant wave that rolled under her keel made her pop, creak, and moan as if the devil himself was trying to tear her guts out. Standing in the main corridor, looking down the length of the vessel you could see the tremendous stress the vessel was undergoing, every wave that ran under her keel caused her to flex so badly that it looked as if she must break her back. When the stern was on one wave and the bow on another, it looked as if you were standing in a valley, and as the wave ran under her, a ripple in her bottom would race toward you until you were seemingly, standing on top of a hill, with the bow and stern hanging below you. How the anchors held and she didn't break her back in those seas no one will never know. A little after one in the morning, the captain and I were in the radio room, trying to get a weather forecast update, when there was a tremendous crash and screeching sound from just aft of the radio room.

We rush down the passageway to the stern of the ship where there was a hatch with a porthole that exited under the helideck (the helideck was located 50 feet above the water line).

We arrived just in time to see what remained of a wave rushing under the ship having just broken the helideck in half. This wave, in order to get on top of the helideck with enough weight and force to destroy it, had to be a monster (It was later reported to have been recorded as the 100-year wave i.e. 100 feet high.)

Shortly after that, the winds started to drop and soon were down to literally, a gentle breeze. The seas began falling rapidly and by six o'clock in the morning it was as if the storm had never existed and was only a figment of our imagination. We may have believed that if it wasn't for the proof of the destroyed helideck, and the reports coming in of disaster all over the North Sea. The one report that stands out in my mind is of a jack-up drilling rig, not too far from the location we were on that was being used as a production platform and serving two SBM (single buoy moorings).

This jack-up had 70 feet of free air space between the water and the bottom of its hull, yet the monster wave had been able to pick up this several thousand-ton drilling rig eleven inches and rotate it six feet, almost tearing the two-pipe line apart that ran to the SBM's (Perhaps that doesn't impress you, but it sure as hell impressed me.)

We finished decompressing the divers that afternoon, and they were fine, glad as hell to be out of the pot with a chance to get a bite to eat, and a breath of fresh air again. Like I said earlier, they really didn't want to talk about their feelings, and even I can understand that they had spent many hours, looking death straight in the face.

Myself, how did I feel? You know, after all these years I can't remember! Maybe its old age creeping up on me, but most likely it's the old brain protecting itself. I have no trouble believing this every time I look into a mirror and see all those grey hairs! And then again maybe it's all those pints and nips because you see I must have lost some of those precious brain cells somewhere along the way. The whole time I was writing the story above, I was trying to remember who the second diver was in that pot with Jock, (a very good friend to this day, even though it been 7 or 8 years since I've seen him). Maybe, if he ever happens to read this, he will give me a call or drop a line and let me know who the other diver was, and then won't I feel a fool when it all comes rushing back and hits me like a ton of shit.

I'm sure someone, somewhere, must have made a cost study of the storm that took place in 1973. I personally don't have a clue, but I do know that now all the major oil companies operating in the North Sea use those criteria to design all their offshore structures, i.e., 100-foot waves and 100-knot winds, so there you have it—the 100-YEAR STORM.

Post War Mines

There are plenty of other ways that can cause near misses besides the weather. There can be fire aboard ship, and that is as serious as a cancer patient with a heart attack. You can have collisions at sea and possibly sink, and there are still a few explosive mines floating around from the last war that may or may not still be active. Any explosive expert will tell you these old mines are very dangerous indeed, as the explosive material itself becomes more sensitive with age, plus the corrosive effect of the salt water may have eroded the arming mechanism to the point that it could fire the mine with the least disturbance. The fact that salt water is corrosive is good in some respects, for if the outer case of the mine does rust through, water is a perfect means of deactivating the explosive. The explosive material is highly hydroscopic but it goes without saying when you come across these potentially dangerous wartime artifacts, you give them as wide a berth as possible. Unfortunately, it's not always possible to avoid being in the near vicinity of one of those devices.

During the war, there were many different types of mines sowed in the North Sea, but the types that we most often encountered were the contact type with horns sticking out from the body of the mine. When these horns were bent or sheared off, they detonated the explosive charge within the mine case. These mines were normally anchored in relatively shallow water with the mine floating under the surface of the water attached to the anchor by a wire rope. These mines were set at different depths to damage or sink vessels of a particular type. Deep enough to let fishing boats and smaller ships pass over them, but a transport or war ship would strike the mines. Since the war, many of the wire ropes anchoring these mines to the seabed have chafed or rusted through, letting the mines pop to the surface and drift with the currents, thus causing a hazard to normal shipping and in our case, the offshore oil industry. But not all of the mines still have their floatation intact, and these lay on the seabed and are tumbled along the bottom in the currents and tides, so that you can encounter these mines on the seabed, long distances from where they were originally laid.

Off the coast of Germany, there are several of these mine fields that have not been completely cleared. These areas are noted on all maritime charts as restricted areas and all shipping is warned to remain well clear of these designated zones.

But all these warnings didn't mean a thing when a particularly nasty storm blew up and the barge that I was on spent 18 hours in one of these mine fields. The wind, seas, currents and tides all combined to force the barge into this field, regardless of having two, large tugboats attempting to tow the barge clear. Maybe you would not consider this to be a near miss, but I can tell you for a fact, the personnel on board certainly considered this a near miss, and you would have felt the same way if you had been on board. I promise you, there was not a single man on that crew who went to sleep. The tension was thick enough to cut with a knife, and 18 hours is plenty of time for nerves to become strung as tight as a bow string. That was one enormously relieved crew when the storm abated and the barge was finally towed clear.

Another incident occurred on what we call a jet barge or bury barge. The function of this type of barge is to excavate a subsea trench under a pipeline to protect and stabilize the pipeline. The trenching is accomplished by the use of a sled that sits over the pipeline and is towed by the barge, which also supplies the high-pressure water to the jets and the air for the airlifts. The combination of these high-pressure jets and the air lift will cut a trench under the pipeline 3 to 7 feet deep, depending on the depth of burial the client requires. The sled is also equipped with load indicators so that the crew on the surface can determine what forces they are exerting on the pipe and also to assist in guiding the sled along the pipeline.

The divers' normal tasks on a jet barge are to set the sled, check the ditch periodically and assist with any problem that may be encountered.

The nature of a jet barge's work, i.e., jetting a trench into the bottom, thus, moving thousands of tons of material a day consisting of sand, silt, and mud, creates a problem for the divers. A large percentage of this material goes into suspension in the water making it impossible for the divers to see anything on bottom after the initial setting of the sled so all their inspection dives are done by feel and feel alone. As I mentioned in Chapter One, "BECOMING A DIVER," a diver's sense of feel is as important as his eyesight on many occasions.

While in the process of burying a pipeline off the coast of Holland, the surface crew recorded abnormal readings from the load cell indicators, which indicated an obstruction between the pipeline and the jet sled. The barge was stopped and the jet sled shut down in preparation for the divers to make an inspection to determine the cause of the high load readings. There was nothing unusual in this occurrence, as the seabed in the North Sea is littered with all sorts of scrap, everything from empty beer cans and fishermen's nets to sunken submarines and battleships so the divers were familiar with these inspection dives to determine the cause of these obstructions. In most cases, these turned out to be a piece of old broken, rusty anchor wire or a small boulder trapped between the pipe and the jet sled.

The divers completed their preparation and the first diver entered the water with the instructions to have a good feel around and let the surface know what the problem was. The diver arrived on bottom and made his way to the front of the sled where he expected to find the object jammed between the pipe and the sled. After a few moments of feeling around he confirmed that there was indeed something jammed at the front of the sled, but he was unable to tell what it was or if he could attach a wire, so the crane could pull the object out from between the pipe and the sled without picking the jet off the pipeline. The diving supervisor asked him to describe what he had found; the diver said that he didn't know what it was but, "It felt like an old anchor buoy about 3 feet in diameter, spherical in shape with a number of short pieces of small pipe welded on to it sticking out at right angles." Well, it didn't take the diving supervisor long for the penny to drop and realize that his diver was having an intimate feeling session with a horned contact mine. The diver was ordered to desist from his feeling activities immediately and prepare to leave bottom.

Now ask that diver if he felt that was a near miss?

As the barge crew waited on tender hooks, the Explosive Ordinance Disposal Team was sent for. On their arrival, they determined that they were unable to do anything to disarm the mine until the jet sled was removed. The crew were all moved to the other end of the barge, and the jet sled was picked off the mine without any drastic effects to the jet sled or the pipeline, but I understand that there were some drastic effects on the crew's nerves. They were lucky in this instance because the mine didn't explode, but if it had exploded, the pipeline and jet sled would have been destroyed, and nobody is sure of what would have happened to the barge, but it is certain that it would have suffered fairly severe damage with possible injury to some of the crew members. Ask them if they thought it was a near miss?

I've had another encounter with the same type of mine as described above, i.e., a horned contact mine. This encounter took place on the semi-submersible drilling rig I mentioned in the first part of this chapter. When I was still a baby diver, all the divers, including myself, were working on the diving equipment one bright, beautiful day; there was very little wind, no seas, just a large 15-foot, lazy, ground swell. The diving system was located on the cellar deck, which is just below the main deck of the rig. From the cellar deck, you have a 360-degree view of the surrounding ocean and also you can see all of the legs on the drilling rig plus the marine riser and guide wires which run to the BOP (Blow Out Preventer) on the seabed.

During a lull in our activities, one of the divers pointed out that there was some unidentifiable object drifting towards us.

As we stood chatting, watching this object slowly drift closer to the rig, speculating on what it may be, it became apparent that what we were looking at was, in fact, a horned contact mine. One of the divers ran to call the captain. As we watched the mine, it was obvious that if the mine maintained its present course and speed, it would be inside the rig within a few minutes.

The captain arrived, and seeing the mine drifting towards us, ordered a work boat launched in order to try to divert the mine away from the rig. However, it was now clear that there was not sufficient time for the boat to be launched and do anything about the mine, before it was in amongst the vessel's numerous legs, columns, sea water intakes, discharge pipes, the marine riser and guide wires.

A feeling of hopelessness overcame all of us as we stood powerless watching the mine drift straight into one of legs, knowing that if it made contact, that there was a very real possibility we would be swimming for our lives in the next few minutes. There was not even time to launch the lifeboats and abandon ship.

As we watched transfixed, the large ground swell launched the mine straight at the leg. This is that moment in time, if you are a religious sort of person, you make your peace with your god. As for me, I do not profess to believe in an almighty, but this moment seemed an appropriate time to practice the recommendation issued by the Atomic Energy Commission, that reads "In the event of imminent nuclear attack, remove all sharp objects from your pockets, remove your spectacles, take cover under the nearest protection, bend over and place your head between your knees and kiss your ass goodbye." As that ugly mine with its grotesque horns protruding from its rusty shell was flung at the leg from the powerful surge of the swell, we all knew that the shit was about to hit the fan, and there was not a thing anyone in the world could do to stop it from smashing into the leg and sending all of us on a trip that we didn't have reservations for.

In the split second before the mine crashed into the leg, the sea intervened and came to our rescue. The backwash of the swell grabbed that artifact of war, a symbol of mankind's foolishness, and guided it around the rig's leg.

There was a huge sigh of relief by one and all, but the ordeal was not over, because we went through the same experience several more times before the mine finally drifted completely through the rig's many legs etc. It even drifted straight through the marine riser and the six guide wires, without touching one. And to top all that off, when the Navy arrived a few hours later to deal with the mine, it was found to be unlike the one in the previous tale. This one proved to be very alive indeed, for when they blew it up several miles away, we saw the geyser of water shoot several hundred feet into the air, and the crash of thunder that reached our ears told us we were very lucky indeed that the sea, our friend, and ally in this case, had seen fit to come to our salvation.

Ask me if I think that was a near miss, and my answer is, "You bet your sweet ass that was a near miss."

Although the following incident was not really a near miss, I felt you might find it of interest, and this seemed like an appropriate place to tell the tale since we are on the subject of mines.

One of Norway's major oil companies laid a pipeline across the Norwegian Trench a couple of years ago, after many years of study as this was one if not the most difficult projects ever attempted in the North Sea.

The Norwegian Trench is a natural geological feature of the North Sea, following just offshore of the Norwegian coastline. The trench, in the area where the pipeline was routed, averaged close to 1000 feet deep. The trench had been a thorn in the side of the Norwegian Government ever since oil was discovered off the coast of Norway in the late 1960s, as the trench prevented Norway from running a pipeline from their offshore oil fields to the beach where it could be processed. Being without a pipeline created many problems in terms of the logistics required; there were oil tankers to ship the oil to shore in offshore storage facilities, and the offshore loading buoys required to load the oil into the tankers, then there were the harbor offloading facilities as well. As you can imagine, this made the cost of producing their oil very expensive. All these problems were found because the technology did not exist until recently to lay large diameter pipelines at those water depths. Of course, all the above background information does not really have anything to do with the following tale, but I thought you might find it of some interest.

The pipeline project consisted of two pipelines to be laid over two seasons, crossing the trench twice. The first season progressed without a hitch, and the third generation lay barge that was selected for the project set five new records in the process.

The second season started in the same spectacular fashion with this giant lay barge spewing pipe off the stinger aft at a phenomenal rate. Dead in the middle of the Norwegian trench they came to a screeching halt when the survey vessel proceeding the lay barge reported that they had picked up several contacts on the side scan sonar that looked like that they should be investigated further.

I would like it to be noted here that the client had spent several million dollars having the pipeline route surveyed prior to commencement of the laying operations. This is very important because when they applied to the government for the permit to lay the pipeline, the government issued the permit with a stipulation that the route was only to be two hundred meters wide, and the pipeline must be laid in the center of that corridor, with an error tolerance of only, +/- 25 meters. When you think of the pipeline in a thousand feet of water not touching down on the seabed for almost a mile behind the barge, these limits start to look pretty small e.g., a flea on an elephant's ass.

As the lay barge that was costing several hundred thousand dollars a day waited, the survey vessel launched its Remote-Control Vehicle (ROV) and commenced a television inspection of these unidentified targets. As the ROV was maneuvered into position on the first target, what should appear on the television monitor in living color, but a grotesque horned contact mine. As the Survey Vessel continued the inspection of the other targets, it turned out that there were almost thirty of these mines located inside the pipeline corridor for one kilometer, with an undetermined number outside the corridor but still inside the Lay Barge's anchor pattern.

Researching of the Department of Defense's archives revealed that during the First World War, there were between sixty and seventy thousand British and American made mines laid between Norway and the Shetland Islands. And here we had found the ones sown in the Norwegian Trench. The mines were not designed to be laid in this depth of water, so the floatation compartments had imploded from the hydrostatic pressure encountered at these depths—in excess of four hundred and forty pounds per square inch (440 PSI). Most of the experts believed that these mines, having laid on the seabed in a thousand feet of water for at least sixty-five years, would all be inactive, but they were not willing to stake their reputations and to categorically state that the mines were harmless. Thus, there was no alternative but to render the mines safe.

This was accomplished by using the ROV to place a small explosive charge on the mines to detonate the explosive inside the mine if it was still active. It is just as well for the experts that they didn't stake their reputations on this little exercise because several of the mines went off with a high order bang.

The clearing of the pipeline corridor took several days to complete and was a very expensive operation. There was no way that the time could be taken to clear the lay barge's anchor pattern, as its pattern was over four miles in diameter and would have taken months to accomplish. There was no way that they could take the chance of picking up a mine in one of the anchor wires and having it come in contact with the barge as the anchors were pulled in. So, the man in charge of the project came up with an ingenious method of crossing the mine field.

The fore and aft anchors were set in the cleared corridor and eight, large, maneuverable tugboats were employed—four to each side of the lay barge, to act as its breast anchors. This method worked flawlessly, and the mine field was successfully negotiated without any mishaps. And today, Norway has its pipelines ashore, after many long years of waiting.

The above tale shows you that when dealing with explosives, you must always treat them as if they can kill you, because they sure as hell will if you give them a chance.

The "Pressure" Of The Norwegian Trench

If you remember earlier, I mentioned the Norwegian Trench. What I did not mention was:

The year was 1982. In fact, the actual date was 26th October 1982.

We were working with Norskhydro, who were looking to lay a pipeline between the U.K and Norway. If you recall the depth of this trench was in the region of 1100 feet.

As with most jobs, Norskhydro needed diving coverage, just in case anything went wrong.

I was skeptical about doing such a deep dive but was convinced by the company that I was working for that I was the man for the job.

Since the go ahead was given, I had to assemble a team of seven divers and a full crew for a workup (a live dry run). The team consisted of divers from the USA, UK, and Norway. Now assembling a crew and getting everything ready is no easy task. It is not like jumping in a car and turning the key. People had to be flown in from all around the world.

The diving system that was to be used was located in New Orleans, purpose built to withstand the depths of the Norwegian Trench. In fact, 1500 feet was the rated depth. The divers were all SAT divers and would be under pressure for two weeks.

Prior to the divers going into the bell, they all had to be checked over by the company doctor. This was routine; we needed to know if anyone had any issues. For you that don't know, if someone requires medical attention, you can't just open the hatch; it would be disastrous. It would take twelve hours for a doctor to be blown down to the same pressure and a further twelve days to get him back to surface pressure. Naturally, as the divers were Deep Sea Diver Extraordinaires, everyone was fit for purpose.

It was decided that the divers would be blown down to 1200 feet, giving a small buffer as the actual depth was closer to 1100 feet. This was a very complex and expensive job. Only one dive was deeper in the world at that time.

Now the job went smoothly and the divers were not required but were retained onboard just in case.

One of the things that come to mind was the expense of the job—for more than one reason. Mainly that it cost $250,000, but

Author, Ledford, prior to the Trench dive in Norway.

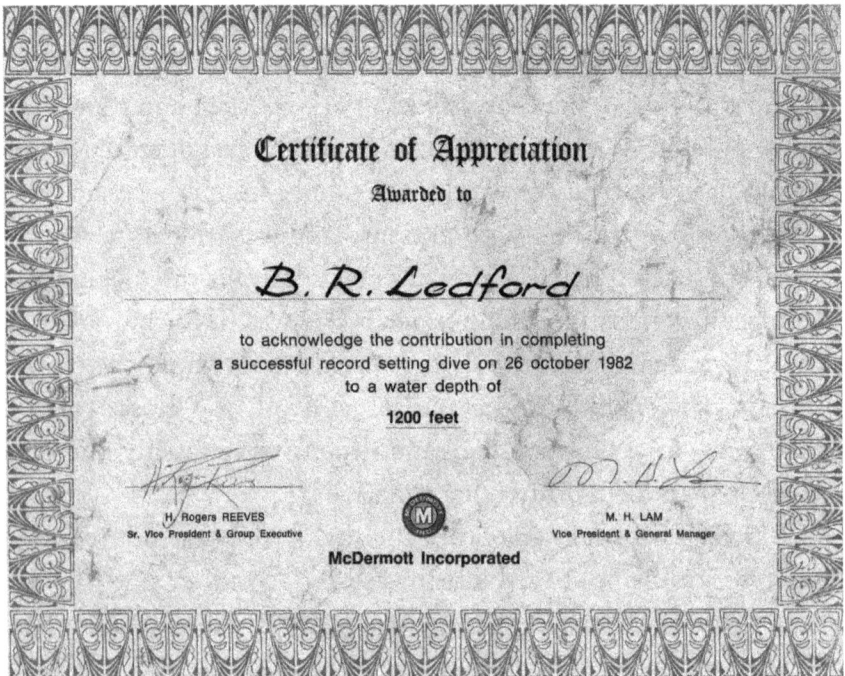

Certificate of Appreciation

Awarded to

B. R. Ledford

to acknowledge the contribution in completing
a successful record setting dive on 26 october 1982
to a water depth of

1200 feet

H. Rogers REEVES
Sr. Vice President & Group Executive

M. H. LAM
Vice President & General Manager

McDermott Incorporated

secondly that every cent was accounted for, and I mean every cent. Now this may not seem like that much money today but remember this was 1982.

Just a little technical information for you:

At 1200 feet, the divers were on a mixture of: oxygen, helium and a dab of nitrogen. If my memory serves me correctly, it was 2% oxygen, 98% helium and as I said a touch of nitrogen.

How does this compare when on the surface, you ask?

So, the air we breathe is 20-21% oxygen, 78-79% nitrogen. So, a big difference. The interesting fact here is at 16% oxygen at sea level you will start to feel the effects of hypoxia. This is when the brain is starved of oxygen and the critical thinking part stops working properly. You can't solve simple tasks, you will try and put a square peg in a round hole.

Not only that, if you go to 10% Oxygen, you would be DEAD.

The real reason I wanted to add this, was for this funny story:

As you know the diving bell was located in New Orleans and that the divers would be under pressure for two weeks. What I did not mention was the bell was on the dock at the time. Now this plays a large part of the story.

As you may or may not know, that when you have a diving bell at 1200 feet of pressure sitting on the dock, the outside pressure remains at sea level. The divers were in the bell for two weeks, so naturally normal bodily functions take place. The wastewater from the bell had to be emptied daily.

To safely achieve this, a number of valves had to be opened in a specific sequence, prior to the main valve. This allowed for the now "pressurized" waste to be brought up from 1200 feet to sea level and then the waste dumped into the main sewer line.

Every morning the site superintendent around 7 a.m., would head to the can to read the paper and drink his coffee. Remember our old friend Murphy's law? Well Murphy decided to pay a visit to that unsuspecting superintendent.

A young, rookie crew member, we will call him Kevin, was working that morning and had to empty the septic tank. Remember all those shiny valves Kevin had to turn? Well, Kevin for whatever reason, maybe did not know, or maybe he did not care or maybe he just wanted to see what would happen. Whatever the reason, Murphy was well and truly in full swing. Kevin opened the main valve.

Can you imagine what was going to happen next?

Yep, just like your favorite soda when you drop a Minto or two into it. . . .

Yes, the pressure was so great that all the human waste shot through the pipes into the main sewer line, at such high pressure, it had to go somewhere and somewhere else it did go. Remember that unsuspecting superintendent reading his newspaper sitting on the can? He was blown clean off, britches around his ankles, paper and coffee mug in hand . . . , the pressure so great the toilet shattered.

From that day onwards, the superintendent vowed never to come in early.

CHAPTER

SIX

The Navy Frogmen

Here is the story that George told me in his own words of how he got involved in diving, what the training was like, and what he thought and felt. Well, to hell with it, here it comes. I will offer you the opportunity of skipping this chapter and save yourselves from being bored for the next hour or so. There is nothing that George enjoys more than talking about himself. His tale may take a while to tell so if you continue to read on, it's no one's fault but your own.

George started out by explaining the differences between a Fairy Tale and a Sea Story.

So, THIS IS NO SHIT, "I was running the streets, wild and crazy doing not one constructive thing with my life. I had dropped out of college and was partying and having a good time drinking beer and chasing women but I can't seem to remember ever catching any of them. One day, I woke up and asked myself what the hell was I accomplishing? All I was doing was wasting time and

I decided I really didn't want to go back to college. I wanted to do something exciting. I had met a guy a few weeks before who had convinced me that if you wanted excitement, the Navy was the place to find it. So, old dumb ass me, I rushed down to my local Navy Recruiter and signed on the dotted line to go and serve God and Country for four years.

"The next several months were spent in basic training learning all the things you are supposed to know to go to sea and be a sailor. Let me say, it certainly opened this young punk's eyes; I learned in a hurry that the sun didn't rise and set on my young ass, which up to then, I had always imagined that it did. Those first few weeks, I sure wished I had listened to the old man, the doctor and my smart-ass brother, the wiser-than-thou lawyer and stayed in college.

"Those few months passed very rapidly, not leaving any great impression on my mind. The thing about basic training that does stand out in my mind was the evening that a team of UDT (Underwater Demolition Team) men arrived at the camp on a recruitment tour. Here was the cream of the navy, the heroes of my dreams, real frogmen, just like the ones I had seen in the movies— bronze golden tans, muscles bulging, and confidence seemingly exuding from them.

"It was explained to us bootcamp scum that this was an experiment as never in the past had they recruited possible candidates from the ranks of trainee sailors. Always in the past, a man was required to have spent at least four years in the Navy before he could be considered as a likely candidate for U.D.T. Training.

"These men gave such a graphic and eloquent recruitment spiel that I was hooked. How could anybody in their right minds not be impressed. All you had to do was volunteer and 17 weeks later you would be just like them, a hero, a real live frogman. Oh, if I had only known. But how could I resist all the vivid pictures they painted of diving in all the oceans of the world; the beautiful submarine seascapes that were just waiting for me to come along and discover. And all the lovely explosives that I would get to play with. Just imagine all the things that I would get to blow to smithereens. Even the descriptions of the physical exertions required on my part could not dissuade me from wanting to be a frogman. I could already see myself—those girls that used to turn up their noses at me, would think differently when I was a superhero.

"When the spiel was finally over and a request for anyone wanting further info to remain behind, I thought that I would be one of the few that remained. But boy, was I in for a surprise because it sure looked like I wasn't the only one who wanted to be a hero, as a matter of fact, it didn't look like anyone left.

"After waiting for what seemed to be hours, I finally had a chance to come face to face with one of the bronze gods. The first

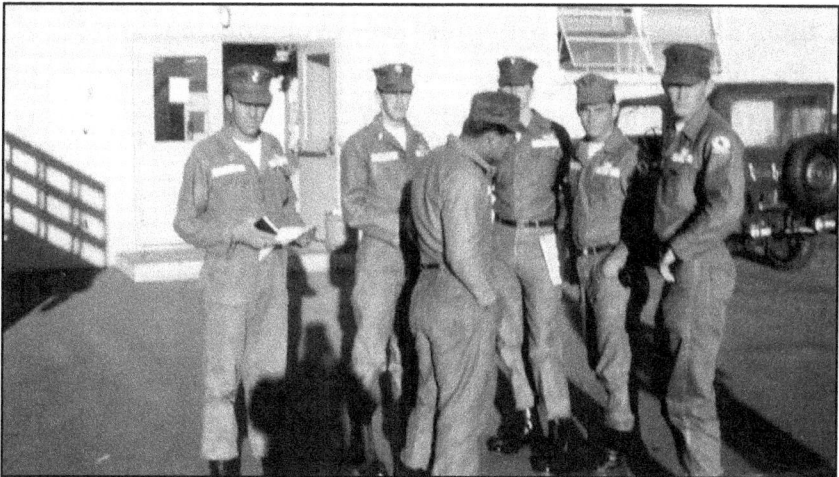

Taken in Coronado, California, the UDT Frogmen Squad is standing around. Author, Billy Ray Ledford, is taking the photo.

question he asked me was why I wanted to become a frogman? I answered him with some line of bullshit along the lines of wanting to serve my Country and God, and this seemed like the best way to accomplish that goal. The man just stared me in the eyes, then said, 'Look asshole, forget the snow job and tell the truth. You are here because you think being a frogman is a glamorous thing to do and you think it will impress the girls. Right?' Well, he had me figured out to a 'T' so knowing that I had blown the interview, I admitted that he was right and expected to be chucked out on my ass. But he said, 'Now we are getting somewhere, drop down and give me 50.' I'm thinking fifty what, when he says, 'Fifty push-ups numb nuts.' Well, I thought I was in good shape, but those 50 push-ups damn near killed me. I should have known then what was in store but I had stars in my eyes; I was going to be a frogman. When the interview was over, he instructed me to report a week later to the swimming pool where they would conduct the preliminary physical fitness and swim tests. Boy, I felt great. I thought I was in.

"When I arrived at the pool expecting to be just one of many, I thought I must have gotten the date wrong or something; there were only a dozen guys there. As it turned out, we were the only ones selected for the swim test out of almost 200 men who had been interviewed. Well, let me tell you, that made me feel pretty good, a real macho man. I puffed out my chest and was ready to whip the world single-handed.

"Well, the UDT men arrived and the officer-in-charge explained the tests that were going to be given, simple, all we had to do was swim 400 yards in less than 11 minutes. Hell, I was no great swimmer but even a child could swim 400 yards in less time than that. Then he explained that we would only swim 100 yards at a time and had to swim four different strokes for each section: 100 yards backstroke, 100 yards breaststroke, 100 yards sidestroke, and

100 yards freestyle and that we would be required to do a few light exercises between the swimming of each different stroke.

"But first, a few calisthenics to warm up. After about an hour and a half of the hardest session of calisthenics we had ever been through in our lives, we were dropping from sheer exhaustion. Our instructors then informed us we were now warmed up and ready to swim that little old 400 yards. Each of us had an instructor to time our swim and to give us a few light exercises between each stroke. I guess so we wouldn't stiffen up from all that cold water.

"All I have to say is, you try swimming 400 yards in 11 minutes, when after every 50 yards you have to get out of the pool, do as many belly stretchers, good morning darlings, and push-ups as you can, and if you were looking a little too strong, you would find a 200-pound instructor sitting on your shoulders while you were trying to do push-ups. Well, I survived that ordeal and did manage to get under 11 minutes by a frog fuzz (no pun meant).

"After these few simple tests were over, each of us hopefuls were interviewed once again. I was told by the instructor that I was the piss poorest specimen of a man that he had ever seen in his life, and what the hell made me think that I had a chance to be a frogman, one of the elites of America's finest fighting men. After this interview, I left with my tail between my legs, feeling like a worm, having been told I would find out in due course how I had done.

"When basic training was finally over and orders were being issued to us new sailors, there had been no word that I had been accepted to UDT Training. As a matter of fact, I had given up hope—after all, what hope does a WORM have.

"You can imagine my elation when my orders were read out by our Officer in Charge. Seaman Second Class Blowhard, George A. to report to the Naval Amphibious Base, Coronado, California, to commence UDT training. It didn't even affect my inflated ego when the officer commented that anybody who volunteered for that type of duty must have a screw loose. And what even added to my elation and expanded my ego even further, was when I learned that there was only one other man besides myself who had been selected to commence training out of the almost 200 original applicants. Only the two of us had survived the final selection."

George said that if he had known at this point what he had let himself in for, he would have put on his seven league boots and disappeared into the sunset.

So, George reported to Coronado Island, one of the most beautiful places in the world—17 miles of silver sand beaches,

Taken in Coronado, California, author, Billy Ray Ledford is on the far left. Beside him is Vanwinkle, Olson, Anderson, and Angle. This photo courtesy the Navy Seal museum in Fort Pierce.

known as the Silver Strand. A land of gentle breezes, waving palm trees, golf courses, plenty of bars and pretty women. After all, it is Southern California and only a few miles from the border of Old Mexico, where one of the world-famous sin cities is located, known as Tijuana. What more could a man like George want.

Unfortunately, George didn't get to sample any of these delights for the next five weeks. They were spent, as his instructors put it, getting into shape. 16 to 18 hours a day exercising, running, and learning to carry and paddle a rubber boat, known as an IBS (Inflatable Boat Small). This IBS you became very attached to because you and your boat crew went absolutely nowhere without it. It was your constant companion, along with your own personal paddle that seem to be grown into your hand. God help the trainee who ever lost one. Because as the old saying goes, "You were up shit creek without a paddle." When those training instructors finished with a man who lost his paddle even his MOTHER wouldn't want him back.

George survived the first four weeks of intense training, and even looks back on this time as a piece of cake compared with what was in store for them in the fifth week. The dreaded "HELL WEEK."

You ask, what's "HELL WEEK?" It is exactly what the name implies, 138 hours of HELL, from 1800 hours Sunday evening till 1200 hours the following Saturday, the trainees are subjected to sheer and utter HELL.

Before I continue with George's tale, I would like to point out some facts that I feel will make you understand a little better what these men subject themselves to. You could discontinue training at any time you felt like, it only required two words and you were gone. No hard feelings, just returned to the regular Navy where you were free to select any course of your choice. These two words were "I QUIT." It was totally up to each individual, whether or not he had the desire to carry on or admit to himself that he wasn't the man he thought he was, a man without the right stuff. The men that didn't have the right stuff were a much higher percentage than you could ever imagine. For example, George's class started with 165 hand-picked men (At the time, the largest class ever to have started a training course). From over 10,000 interviews with possible candidates, these 165 men were finally selected from a shortlist of 1000 men who had been tested mentally and physically and were able to make-up the Navy's finest. Seventeen weeks later, only 24 of the original 165 men graduated from UDT training. These were the men that had the right stuff. So, as you can see, when I refer to UDT training as one, if not the hardest military training in the world, it's not just bullshit.

I hear someone saying, what about the SEALs. I will clue you in. To become a SEAL, you must first complete UDT training. There is no special training for SEALs to try and find that magical thing called the right stuff. Their training is in specialties, cloak and dagger, languages, politics, etc. They are frogmen, trained for clandestine operations. I think now you have a clearer insight into why men who successfully complete UDT training and earn the right to call themselves a frogman, are so proud.

Back to George's tale. "138 hours of sheer hell, 138 hours of being soaking wet, 138 hours of running, carrying and paddling your IBS and most important of all, 138 hours without sleep for most of the men. You see, everything is a competition, a race, a problem, to test your physical stamina and mental agility to determine how you stand up under extreme conditions of stress and sheer exhaustion. After a full day of running, crawling, racing, paddling, etc., at midnight, a further exercise is set up that requires about 6 hours to complete. All the boat crews start at the same time and the crew that completes the course first is allowed to sleep till the last crew comes in. This is your reward for winning, but when you are speaking of men of this caliber, there are only minutes separating the fastest from the slowest. The crew that had the most sleep that hellish week had less than 2 hours. What does this type of cruel, torturous training accomplish? In short, in a crisis, it teaches a man that he has far greater resources of stamina than he ever realized he possessed; a knowledge that will undoubtedly save his life someday and if that doesn't make it worthwhile, nothing will."

Well, George made it over the first big hurdle, which is more than can be said for over 100 of the original men who started training (I think that might be what you call separating the chaff

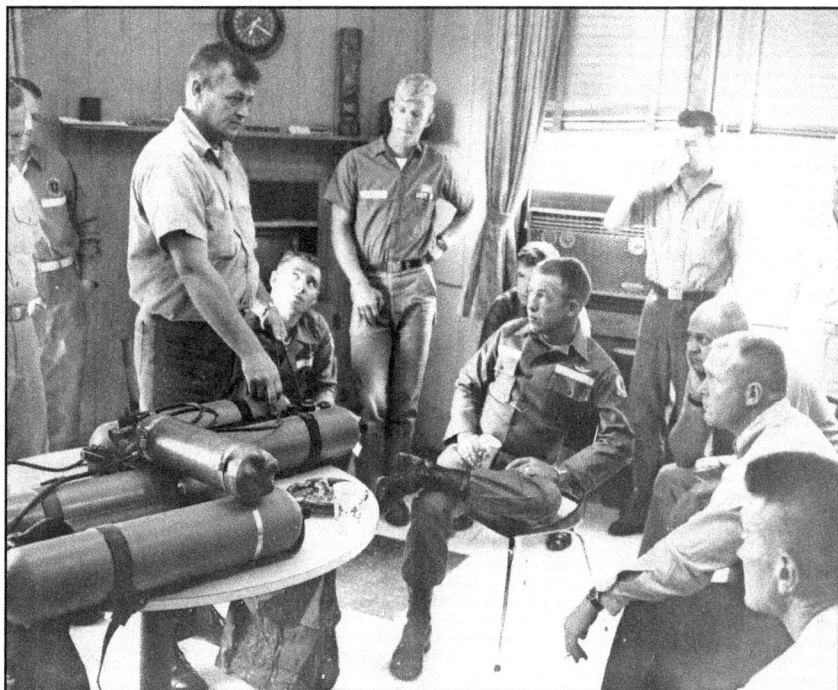

Taken in Washington D.C learning the MK9 gear.

from the grain). In some ways, there were very sad incidents where men who had reached the end of their rope, exhausted and unable to carry on but still full of desire, broke down and cried. Other men showed unbelievable feats of courage, carrying on to complete Hell Week despite having blisters on their feet so bad that their boots were full of blood, or even had blood running down their legs from where their inside thighs were so badly chafed that they have scars to this day.

Human nature is a strange thing indeed. Men who at the beginning of training seemed to have all the right characteristics—the mental and physical strength to carry on—were in actual fact, the first to go. Whereas, some of the men you felt didn't have a snowball's chance in hell of finishing, turned out to be real leaders, virtual towers of strength.

The men who had survived HELL WEEK knew that they had the physical and mental strength to finish training, but, the big but, did they have all the other skills required to complete the full training program, that is to say an academic and educational background that would enable them to cope with the diving medicine and diving physics or math to work out diving tables and explosives formulas. There were also radio communications to be learned, the Morse Code to be mastered, together with Semaphore and Aldis lamp signaling, all the gas laws such as Charles' Law and Boyles' Law, gas mixtures, diving and explosive safety, and marine animals' identification. A thousand and one items of knowledge required, as George said, "Just to be a frogman." For now, they were ready to start the real training. There were going to be four months of 14-16 hours a day of intensive training ahead of them. A large percentage of which was classroom work; at least 8-10 hours a day, every day.

The other training didn't cease. If anything, it became more intense than ever. Daily, there was another qualification that had to be met—open ocean swims of increasing distance with time limits. These swims started at 1 mile building up to 7 miles of open ocean swims. Long distance runs 1-16 miles on the beach and in soft sand that had to be done in less than three hours, and the final one of 24 miles that had to be completed in under four hours.

There was also another, big, outstanding question—did you really have the nerve to do all the things you were required to learn and do in order to graduate? Like, for example, jumping out of a helicopter flying at 60 knots 60 feet above the sea. Did you really want to be a diver?

Did you really want to play with those live explosives? Did you really want to be trained to swim into an enemy beach to do a recce while they shot live bullets at you? Did you really want to lock out of a submarine at sea and hope you could find it when you needed to? Plus, after you graduated from UDT training, there were more schools waiting for you, like jump school—anyone would have to be a fool to jump out of a perfectly good airplane anyway.

There was arctic survival, jungle survival, desert survival (where you ate rats and rattlesnakes, or you didn't eat), ranger school, ski school. And if you really liked to live dangerously, there was always EOD (Explosive Ordinance Disposal) school where you could learn to take apart some bomb that someone else had tried their best to put together in such a manner as to make it very uncomfortable for you to take apart. Life expectancy in regard to reaching a ripe old age was not very promising.

But even considering all the things that you are required to learn, diving was still the most important. It was the one that your life really depended on. It was the one that would get you into an enemy harbor and out again. In order to be able to do this, it was necessary to learn to use Closed Circuit Diving Equipment. This is the most dangerous diving gear that you can use because it uses pure oxygen as a breathing medium, and oxygen under pressure is deadly poisonous if you exceed certain depth limitations. The reason for using oxygen in a closed-circuit system is that there are no air bubbles exhausted to the surface to give away your position, plus these systems are almost totally silent, so your presence is that much harder to detect on underwater listening devices.

It was necessary to learn how to repair and maintain these diving rigs, to know the proper procedures to set them up so they would function properly, and, as these were closed-circuit systems, you required a method to remove the carbon dioxide that your body dispelled. This was done by using a cannister in the system that your expired gas passed through. This cannister was filled with a chemical that would remove the carbon dioxide, and unlike today, the chemicals that we used in the early sixties could be highly toxic if swallowed and were even caustic in some cases. For example, if your cannister became flooded and you happened to drain this solution onto your balls.

So, needless to say, diving in these units was not the safest thing that one could do. We lost many more fellow comrades to diving accidents than to any other causes of death. But this was the military, and you were expected to take risks and anyway you knew that it couldn't happen to you. (In four years, out of the two teams on the West Coast, which consisted of just under 200 men, there were 7 fatal accidents, and when you look at those kinds of odds, it's not the best business in the world to be in.) Since I mentioned that there were two teams on the West Coast, I would like to go ahead and point out that at the time there were four UDT teams in the Navy—the two on the West Coast—Teams 11 and 12, on the

East Coast—Teams 21 and 22. There were also two SEAL TEAMS. Teams 1 and 2, one stationed on each Coast.

The total number of men in all six of these teams never exceeded 600 hundred men as, in theory, each team was supposed to have a 100 man complement, but they were always under complemented. I don't know the actual figures, but I would guess that there were never more than 500 frogmen in the Navy at any given time.

I don't want to confuse you regarding Navy divers. In addition to the UDT and Seal Teams, there were numerous other divers in the Navy: there were salvage divers, ships divers, EOD divers, test divers, rescue divers, scuba divers, etc. I suppose several thousand in all. These divers were the real workhorse divers of the Navy; they were the equivalent of commercial divers in the oil fields.

Whereas a UDT diver was a warrior. He was the first one on the beach, and even sometimes days in advance of a beach assault. These men were dropped by submarine to sneak ashore and conduct reconnaissance to determine the enemy's strength, weakness, numbers, locations, their defenses, etc., He then would have to make his way, undetected, back offshore to rendezvous with a submarine that may or may not show up. Like I said, if there was a beach assault, they were the first ones to the beach, surveying and destroying any obstacles that may hinder an amphibious assault. These activities took place directly under hostile fire and could definitely be considered hazardous to your health. A little pun the frogmen were using several decades before the tobacco industry was forced into putting that phrase onto every pack of cigarettes they sell. I digress, back to George's tale.

"Over the next few months, our numbers slowly dwindled. Men who couldn't meet the qualifications required for all the various tests, both physical and mental, fell by the wayside. At this stage of training, there were no second chances, either you succeeded or you were gone. A mistake was unforgivable. There was one pair of trainees that were dropped during the very last week of training with only three days to complete training. They committed the cardinal sin—lost their haversack of explosives while swimming into the beach to load an obstacle. They were gone so fast that no one even had a chance to commiserate with them. Your health was your problem; you did everything humanly possible to maintain yourself in a state of health. Sickness was no excuse for not being able to keep up. If you had a disabling accident you were finished. All the weeks and months of grueling training down the drain. Which reminds me of one of the men who was in training with me. He decided to go to town one night and have a few beers. As it turned out, he got into a fight for some reason or other and wound up with a broken jaw, so with only one month to graduation he was dropped from training. He was one very sick at heart man, but he had the right stuff and entered the next training class and went through HELL all over again; this time he stayed out of bars until he graduated.

"Well, finally all those months of training were behind us and we were approaching the final climax, which was the last two weeks of training. We travelled offshore to a Military Training Island called San Clemente where we spent those two weeks living rough and putting into practice all the skills we had acquired over the last five months, and then finally the big day arrived. The day that we were to become fully fledged navy underwater demolition team members. This was a day I will not forget until the day I die, and I'm positive that my fellow class members recall it just as vividly as I do.

"As I looked around me on that memorable day and saw only 34 of the original 165 men who started training, it dawned on me

Amphibious Training Command   United States Pacific Fleet

Naval Amphibious School

United States Navy

This is to certify that LEDFORD, Billy R., SA, 597 17 10, USN

has satisfactorily completed the prescribed course of instruction in

Assault Boat Coxswain (L-4) (excluding Survival-in-Water, SW-1) on 1 February 1963

B. HASHWALL, Commander   U. S. Navy
By direction

Commanding Naval Amphibious School

1IND-PHIPAC-1500/1 (10-61)

Amphibious Training Command   United States Pacific Fleet

Naval Amphibious School

United States Navy

This is to certify that LEDFORD, Billy R., SA, 597 17 40, USN

has satisfactorily completed the prescribed course of instruction in

Underwater Demolition Training (H-6) 13 August 1962 to 10 December 1962

B. HASHWALL, Commander   U. S. Navy
By direction

Commanding Naval Amphibious School

1IND-PHIPAC-1500/1 (10-61)

what an extraordinary feat we had accomplished. And to this very day, I remember each and every one of my classmates. They are not the type of men that you could forget, even if you wanted to."

George then said to me, "You asked me why I have always been so proud to have been a frogman, do you understand why now?" and I had to answer that I most surely did. But now I was more convinced than ever that he was a nut case.

Now, you too know why George was so proud when he called his father, the doctor, on graduation day to proudly tell him he was a frogman. (See Chapter One, BECOMING A DIVER.)

If you remember, I said George was one of two recruits that were selected from basic training. You may also be wondering how I know in such detail the things George did. It was not that George was not a great storyteller. It was as if I WAS THERE . . .

The Truth About The Evenrude/Mercury Outboard

Class 29 Final Night of Hell Week:

The object on this operation was to paddle from and return to the dock outside of the training office at the south end of San Diego Bay. An all-night operation, keeping in mind this is already approximately 130 hours into Hell Week, which is to say that the crews were totally fucked in more ways than one.

I don't remember all the members of my boat, as those were the early days. We had an enlisted 2nd Class Petty Officer as coxswain who seemed like an old man, maybe thirty years old. There were not enough officers to go around. We were boat crew seven, on which I was a member to the end of training.

Our crew had been the fastest crew throughout training/Hell Week, winning virtually every race. We were issued one of the old-style IBS's, "Big Nasty" and had more patches than you could count. The thing is, we developed a method of propelling this "beast" through the water quite rapidly. Instead of deep strokes, we used shallow quick strokes and that seemed to work very well.

Back to the heart of the story:

Our "friendly" instructors (otherwise known as rotten bastards) decided to have a little fun by securing our boat to the dock. Now when I say secured, I'm not speaking as a sailor would consider properly and shipshape moored, I mean it looked like a demented spider had been turned loose. By the time we had unsnarled the spider web, all the other boat and crews had long since disappeared into the darkness on their merry way to the south end of San Diego Bay.

Like I've said, we were the fastest and proud of the fact, we were determined to catch and pass the other crews. As time passed, we slowly caught and overtook each boat in turn, counting them off one by one until there was only one boat crew left (maybe boat crew six). Still some distance ahead that we could not see or hear them. We increased our effort and chased after them all night, without success.

At about point "Golf", there were moored (properly I hope) some pontoons used for landing craft training. So, the mystery of what happened to boat crew six was that our friendly rotten bastard instructors had called them over and hidden them in the pontoons until all the crews had passed, thus where the rumor of Evenrude/Mercury outboard came from. Of course, boat crew six never fest up and admitted they were lucky assholes to win that night.

What really pisses me off, boat crew six got to secure for the night, hot showers and sweet sleep until the last boat came in. To think we missed out of that slice of heaven because of our friendly instructors (please note that I refrained from calling them rotten bastards).

Last note:

There is no way to describe the hurt and pain of that last night of HELL WEEK, people were so exhausted they had no idea where they were, hallucinating, falling out of the boat. One member swore there was a train coming across the bay.

There is only one way to feel it, you had to have been there.

Frogman's Tackle

The following few paragraphs are some of the humorous things that have happened to Navy frogmen.

One early morning, a Navy diver (frogman) decided to go for a workout on the Silver Strand Beach (So named because of its beautiful silver sands, nothing like pointing out the obvious). It was such a nice, warm, clear morning, it just didn't seem right to be wearing clothes, so off with his gear, a quick dash down the beach to warm up, catch a few big breakers to practice, and polish up on his body surfing techniques and he would be off to a great start for the day.

Unfortunately, just as he was riding that last super wave into the beach, the police arrived and arrested him for indecent exposure on a public beach.

The police were very understanding when he explained that he was just having an early morning workout and didn't think anyone would see him. The policeman said he understood, but he had to arrest him since a woman had filed a complaint that a diver was running up and down the beach naked. He enquired how this lady could possibly know that he was a diver. The policemen explained that they had asked the same question to the lady that since he was nude, how could she identify him as a diver. Her explanation was very simple, "A tall handsome man, a bronze body, BIG WATCH, SMALL COCK."

Even though divers have a reputation for not being overly endowed, I can assure you that there are exceptions to the rule. Two divers come to mind who are hung like the proverbial jackass (here we are back to donkey dicks again).

Here is a "quickie" for you (no, not that type of "quickie"). John, who's hung like a donkey, and very proud of it, almost to the point of being vain, was being loud and boisterous about the size of his tool and pointing out the inadequacy of the other frogmen's sexual equipment, who after all were mere mortals. One of the divers, Pete, who is known for his quick wit and biting remarks, replied, "I wouldn't be so proud of that stick of meat hanging between your legs if I were you, John." When John enquired why, Pete replied, "Because all the divers in the Navy know how big a pussy your WIFE has." Ah, the sweet taste of one-upmanship or as most likely in this case, revenge.

A bunch of us deep sea divers were standing in a pub one afternoon quietly sipping our soft drinks, when an old buddy of mine arrived with another diver dressed like a gentleman (You will just have to take all this bullshit with a grain of salt, because anyone who's ever met a diver knows they don't own any clothes except worn out tennis shoes, pronounced 'tenny' shoes, blue jeans and holey T-shirts, which they most surely got from Goodwill Industries or the Salvation Army, and only then if they couldn't steal them from one of their mates). Well, anyway, my buddy introduced this fine upstanding young diver to me as 'Shitter Brown.' Needless to say, I was totally amazed that anyone would have an as unlikely name as that. I was fairly certain that no mother would ever hang a handle that disgusting on a baby, no matter how much she hated the father (even if he had been a diver and had run away to some great diving job in Timbuktu, leaving her with a bun in the oven). Myself, being very considerate of other people's feelings, waited all of 30 seconds before asking him where or how he got tagged with an uncommon name like, 'shitter.' As I said, since I was so considerate and also very observant of other people's feelings, I could tell right off that he was a bit embarrassed and would prefer not to discuss this particular subject at this moment in time. I could tell by his color change, starting at blushing pink, progressing through what can only be described as purple rage. It really didn't help matters that the other divers had gathered around him like a pack of slobbering wolves closing in on Bambi for the kill. But my old buddy, not being nearly as sensitive to other people's feelings as myself, launched into a very vivid and graphic explanation/display of how poor Mr. Brown had come by his very colorful nickname. Though it was very difficult to hear above all the shouts and hoots of rude laughter, "You motherfucker—I'll kill you for this," plus many more flowery phrases. I was finally able to piece together how Mr. Brown got an unusual name like 'shitter.'

Seemingly, my old buddy and Brown were in the U.S. Navy's underwater demolition teams together (Remember those fearless, fighting, fucking, frogmen). They were living on the base in barracks, and one evening, after a hard day of sunning themselves on the Silver Strand Beach watching the local beach bunnies strolling the sands in their most fetching bikinis, a crowd of our superheroes felt a little run on the town was just the thing to top off a perfect day (Going to town for a few beers is normally referred to as hitting the beach).

To stop some of this bullshit and get on with the story, what started out to be a quiet run ashore to drink a few beers and to chase a little pussy, turned into a Jose Cuervo (tequila) drinking contest, (the foulest of strong beverages that was ever distilled by man. Only the Mexicans would do something like that to the human race).

You know what I'm talking about, you have seen it in the movies, a lick of salt, chuck the tequila down your gullet in one go, a quick bite of lemon to get that shitty taste out of your mouth, plus it helps to wash the tequila out of your throat before it burns through your vocal cords. Then, you do it all over again and again and again, until, you can't do it again. At this point, any man who can still say his name is declared the winner and gets to pay the bar bill because everyone else is in the land of nod. (You guys really thought that I was just going to let the fact pass about whether or not it's salt first, then the tequila, and finally the lemon, or is it the lemon first, tequila next and then the salt, or any combination of all of the above that your alcohol befuddled brain can come up with. If you really want to know the truth, nobody gives a rat shit one way or the other).

You think I digress, well back to the tale then. At the crack of dawn, when that most hated of sounds by all military men, regardless of nationality, race, color or creed—reveille—blared out and our still fearless, non-fucking, still drunk, frogmen began to climb out of their fart sacks, bushy tailed and bright eyed, full of piss and vinegar ready to face another day of being superheroes. It slowly began to dawn on them that there was a vile, horrible stench wafting from the direction of Mr. Brown's bunk. They set out to discover the source of this vile odor. Their investigation proved fruitful indeed, and much to their delight found that the source of the odor was no doubt Mr. Brown's bunk, for there lying in all his glory tucked into a fetal position, balls ass naked, without a care in the world was Mr. Brown, grasping by one end a very large brown turd, with the other end stuck delicately into his ear.

So now, you too know the tale of how Mr. Brown came to be known as Mr. Shitter Brown.

But it is not really the end of the story, because, you see 'Shitter' wasn't exactly happy about people laughing at his misfortune so when the story was over and everybody had gotten off the floor, wiped their eyes and their sides had stopped hurting from all that hilarious laughter, and had recovered some semblance of composure, Shitter said "Piss on you guys, I'm going back to the States, where only a few people still laugh at me whenever they see me." And off he went. But here is the real kicker, my OLD BUDDY told me that a tequila drinking contest had taken place over eight years previously.

I guess there are just some things you can't live down in a dozen lifetimes.

The Last Laugh

Here is a little tale about one of the Navy frogmen who was nicknamed 'Bear Tracks', as you can guess, he was so called because of the size of his feet but let me assure you that his feet were not the only big thing about Bear Tracks. It's true he wore a size 16 shoe, and stood six feet six inches tall, weighed 245 pounds and was hung like that proverbial donkey we keep talking about.

Bear Tracks was a gentleman, if there could be such a thing as a diver being called a gentleman. What to most divers would be their proudest possession, was a constant source of embarrassment to Bear Tracks. The other divers realizing that Bear Tracks was sensitive to his unusually large tool (the same size in fact as his shoe size) took great delight in trying their best to make him even more self-conscious than he already was by making all the rude remarks that they could think of. And divers can think of plenty of cutting remarks. One day, the subject of how uncomfortable Bear Tracks' tool must be restricted inside a tight wetsuit which had no provisions made to accommodate his extra-large wang (that is not wang as in computer) these considerate divers decided to help Bear Tracks with his problem. They went to the drying room and pinched his wetsuit. Using the sleeve cut off from an old wetsuit, they then modified Bear Tracks' wetsuit by cutting out the crotch and then carefully shaping and gluing the sleeve into place between the legs of Tracks' wetsuit. They fashioned Bear Tracks' very own personal lookalike WANG WARMER, even with a bulbous head. Their finished product looked like a two and one-half legged wetsuit.

They then rehung Tracks' suit in the drying room and waited for the next dive, anticipating with great delight the expression on Bear Tracks' face when he discovered the new addition to his wetsuit.

A few days later, the team was called out on a bitter cold night to do a simulated sneak attack on one of the Navy's warships to check the ship's defensive alertness for attempted underwater attack, in case of hostile aggression. There is nothing uncommon about those types of operations—they are part of the Navy frogmen's everyday job.

The predive briefing was finished and all the divers retired to the drying room to get their wetsuits. All the divers were slyly watching Bear Tracks for his reaction when he discovered that his suit had been extensively modified. But, to their surprise, he showed no reaction whatsoever, as a matter of fact, they saw that his wetsuit was in a perfect state of repair with the giant tool holder removed and the hole professionally patched with an artful diamond shaped patch insert.

They then got to see Bear Tracks' reaction, for he roared with laughter as each and every member of the team discovered, with shocked horror, that their wetsuits had a large diamond shaped hole cut into the crotch!

That was one of those times when the diver's prank completely backfired. As Tracks loved to tell, "the size of the divers' proudest possessions when they came out of the freezing cold water that night, would have embarrassed his two year old son."

The saying goes, ". . . he that laughs last, laughs loudest."

Above: UDT standing around and/or laying in the sun. Picture is of Payne (squad buddy of author, Ledford). Taken in California. Below: Divers and crew standing around being lazy, resting against a Diver Delivery Vehicle (DDV).

CHAPTER
SEVEN

Gorilla Theater

If you ever asked a diver if he was queer, one of two things would possibly happen. He would knock you on your ass and kick the shit out of you or throw his arms around you and stick 9 fathoms of passionate tongue down your throat.

I'm sure they are out there but having been in the diving business for over 20 years, I can honestly say I've never met anyone whom I knew for certain was a faggot diver. But when you get three or four divers together in a respectable restaurant, or a high-class night club or pub, I can guarantee you that they will bust their asses to prove that they are as queer as a nine-dollar bill (They will expend only slightly less energy if it's a spit and sawdust joint). Why do they do this? Let me assure you, it's for one reason and one reason only, and that's SHOCK. There isn't anything that gives these demons of the depths more sheer pleasure and enjoyment, except drinking beer and chasing pussy, than shocking John Doe Public, by performing a few acts of gorilla theater. These impromptu performances, in most cases, follow the normal pattern of boy meets boy, boy falls in love with boy, boys start getting it on. All to the horror and shock of the locals. There are many themes and variations of this particular script, but the most effective is when the scenario is set up in such a fashion that some of the locals unwittingly become supporting characters. You wouldn't believe the star quality performances some of these poor unsuspecting actresses/actors/suckers are capable of delivering. I mean like real emotions, tears and would you believe—violence.

Not all of these performances are Oscar winners, nor are they all based on the poofter/faggot's theme. Some of the more successful themes are, Boy meets Boy, occasionally Girl meets Girl (depending on how primed you've gotten the ladies on Babycham. What? I hear you say, with disbelief in your voice. Well, you don't really believe these sweet lovable creatures would consume anything stronger than Babycham, do you)? And then there is the irate husband; this is the real showstopper but you must have an accomplished gorilla theater cast to pull this one off and stay out of jail.

One recommendation that I would suggest, if you decided to attempt any of the following performances yourself, is that you liberally apply (internally) 100 proof alcohol, straight or diluted, with another liquid substance of your choice to your cast. This ancient remedy, usually referred to as Dutch courage, will help break down those first night jitters and to rid the cast of inhibitions that would otherwise affect their performance. Plus, it deadens the pain when some angry sucker catches on to what you are up to and smashes you over the head with a pint mug. And if your little sham doesn't come off, you will be rip-roaring drunk and won't give a shit anyway.

This little performance took place a number of years ago in Antwerp, that little city of sin in Belgium, not noted for its tulips, but almost as well-known as Amsterdam for its houses of ill repute, you know, whorehouses. (Don't get all excited this story is not about whorehouses and the ladies of the night.) This story is about Gorilla Theater in a bar in the red-light district of Antwerp.

A crowd of our deep-sea diving heroes arrived in Antwerp after a lengthy offshore trip full of the proverbial piss and vinegar, raring to hit the beach and raise some hell, maybe even kick ass and take names. Hell, who knew, one might even get a strange piece of pussy.

So, our heroes showered, shit, shaved, shined their tenny shoes, and put on their cleanest, dirty shirt (Tee), grabbed a handful of money, called a taxi, instructed the driver to take them where the action was happening. Telling any taxi driver in Antwerp to take you where the action is only means one thing to him—head for the red-light district. (That's what our heroes meant anyway).

Of course, there was no way in hell to get past that first pub after being offshore for three months. The driver finally understood that they wanted to stop for some reason and pulled over in front of the pub. No sooner had the taxi stopped rolling but out piled the boys, saying to the driver "keep the meter running, we'll be back in a minute."

After a couple of hours of tossing back a few brews, our boys were primed and ready to hit it, so back into the taxi and down to that area of illicit pleasures. When they arrived, they paid off the taxi; hell, it only cost a week of a miner's pay (chicken feed). And off they charged, looking for all that action. Only to discover that it was some kind of weird holiday and there was about as much action as you would find at a church outing for handicapped old age pensioners in wheelchairs.

A few hours later, around midnight, and we find them sitting in about the sixth or ninth (69) bar still downing beers as if the Belgians were going to close the breweries forever. At about this point, they decided that if there was going to be any action, they were going to have to make it happen themselves. After a number of suggestions that were vetoed as "the most stupid goddamn idea I've ever heard," someone broached the subject of Gorilla Theater. Well, after another hour kicking around different scenarios, it was decided that it was to be Boy meets Boy, but this time it was going to be done with a different twist.

The three main characters in this sham/hoax were Tom, Dick, and Harry. Tom and Dick were to be lovers and Harry was to arrive on the scene and become Tom's rival for Dick's affections (I'm not going to tell you anymore about the scenario now, you will just have to wait until it unfolds).

THE CHARACTERS

Tom: The masculine half of a pair of faggots. Six feet four inches tall, 16 stones, blonde hair, brown eyes and built like a Greek god (A better description would be a dilapidated, weather-beaten, brick shithouse).

Dick: The feminine half of a pair of faggots. Physical description of no importance, he was picked because he was the prettiest, (Actually he was picked because he had the longest hair and looked like a cunt. The truth is, he's as ugly as the North end of a Southbound bull).

Harry: The queer rival of Tom, fat but strong and as mean as a junkyard dog. Harry wasn't selected for this role, he took it.

Now the story starts to unfold. A bar was selected at random. It had a dozen or so people quietly celebrating whatever holiday it was.

Tom and Dick were to enter the bar together, playing their roles as lovers. Harry and the other two divers were to come along a few minutes later, so the people in the bar wouldn't associate them as being together.

And, from this point, about one o'clock in the morning, it was all ad-lib, they played their parts to perfection. It was Gorilla Theater at its finest. Their acting was sly, devious, outrageous, and I will swear on the *U.S. Navy Diving Manual*, with King Neptune as my witness, that not a single person left that bar until the performance had reached its final climax when the little hand was on six and the big hand was on eleven.

There is no way in hell that I can even remember all the details of that glorious performance, but I will attempt to portray a whiff of the atmosphere these sham/hoax artists created in that pub on that obscure Belgian holiday.

Tom and Dick, the two poofs, were cuddling on the other side of bar from where Harry and his mates were sitting having a quiet chat sipping their beers. The other customers were watching our two lovers but were not particularly shocked. After all, this is Belgium and gays are not an uncommon sight. Harry even began to chat up a bird at the bar who was alone and just a little past her prime. In the meantime, Dick starts making eyes at Harry who responds to these forward advances which pisses Tom off because this guy is making a run on his guy; and all the time, Harry's new conquest is trying to get him to leave Dick alone because, after all, he can have her and what does a big, strong, handsome man like him want to have anything to do with another man.

By this time, several hours into the act, the other customers (Our unsuspecting audience and supporting cast), have split about down the middle with half on Tom's side and the other half on Harry's, with all of them against that slut, Dick, who is playing two men off against each other. Of course, 'That Slut' is in all his glory, coyly tossing his hair, and fondling his glass as if it was a phallus symbol, totally enjoying his gay, queer, poof, faggot-self. And there is the bartender standing behind a look of bewilderment on his face. He thought he had seen everything, but this was a different kettle of fish all together.

His customers are screaming and shouting at each other and on the verge of going to fisticuff city. Two giant faggots, who looked like they should be rough, tough, deep-sea divers instead of queers are pushing and shoving each other, about to knock themselves senseless over some long, greasy-haired, ugly as sin, queen. There is that goddamn stupid bar fly crying her eyes out because that fat ass prefers to make it with boys instead of her. And to top it all, those two assholes down at the other end of the bar who came in with fat ass are laughing so hard they can't even stand up. "Fuck this shit; I'm calling the Police."

Well, there you have it; Gorilla Theater at its finest. But the shit didn't really hit the fan until our boys started slapping hands giving each other "five." Patting themselves on the back and congratulating each other on how they really got those suckers because that is when those suckers joined forces and would have torn our heroes into little bitty pieces, if they hadn't run like hell. How about that—they didn't ride slowly off into the sunset like in the movies, but they did run like hell into the sunrise.

The One With The Uninvited Guest

Here is a boy meets boy, with a little help from girl meets girl:

Bob, Carol, Ted, and Alice who were always chumming around together were sitting in a pub one afternoon minding their own business trying to decide what type of mischief they could get up to when a local gent joined their table uninvited.

The stranger proceeded to listen to their conversation with avid interest. He ignored any comments made that he would probably be more comfortable at some other table, and the prick sat there being obnoxious in a silent, leering manner. He was obviously enjoying himself being rude to these young, beautiful (sic) couples.

Well, Bob and Ted launched into a queer routine in the hope of shocking this asshole into leaving. Even though they were playing fairly convincing roles, this prick just rolled his eyes as if to say, "I've seen it all before," and that is when the ladies came to the rescue. Carol says to this asshole, "Oh, isn't that just terrible, look at those two, I just can' t stand it." Our asshole buddy is all concerned and lets it be known that he can't stand that despicable type of behavior either. Carol begins sobbing, shoulders shaking in great distress, to see her boyfriend, Bob, hugging and cuddling another man. Our asshole buddy sees his great chance, so he pats Carol on the shoulder and tells her not to worry, that he will take care of her, to which Carol replies, "I don't think you understand," and with a meaningful look at Alice, finishes with, "I want some too" and the girls threw themselves into each other's arms and commence a long passionate kiss.

Well, not only did that asshole leave their table, but also left the bar shouting to the bartender about the perverts he allowed into his establishment. And, oh joy, the bartender was laughing his ass off because he had witnessed the whole scene right from the beginning and knew exactly what they were up to. Not only that, he also gave them free drinks on the house, telling them he had been trying to get rid of that obnoxious prick for months without any success. He was so thick-skinned; he was bulletproof.

So now we can see even Gorilla Theater has some usefulness.

A Drink, A Lover And A Gun

This is on the scenario of the irate husband/lover.

And my advice is don't ever attempt this little stunt unless you don't mind spending a stint in jail because I guarantee the chances are very good that is where you will be receiving your mail.

This little episode took place on the spur of the moment and if all those concerned had been sober at the time, their common senses would probably have prevailed, and they would have realized that this one was better left unperformed.

It all started one Saturday evening when Bob, Carol, Ted, and Alice were sitting around sipping on Harvey Wall Bangers so named because after a couple of them you can bang your head on the wall and not feel any pain. It is a concoction of vodka, Galliano, and orange juice, mixed to proportions that satisfy your particular sadistic tenacity. Ted and Alice were visiting Bob and Carol for the weekend and when Bob asked Ted what he had been up to, Ted told him he had been refereeing a local sporting event where he was the official starter. In fact, he still had his starting pistol in the car, and you wouldn't believe how much it looked like the real thing. Of course, Bob wanted to see this shooting iron and, needless to say, one thing led to other, until they had convinced themselves that it would be fun to go down to their local where they knew everybody and perform a little act of Gorilla Theater for the amusement of the locals. So, they merrily retired to their local, with visions of all the fun they were going to have dancing in their heads.

They entered the pub said "hello" to all the other local drunks and noted that there was a large percentage of strangers present in a very packed room. But they did not let a small thing like that deter them from the pleasure they had anticipated. They launched into their performance.

Standing at the bar, they were quietly arguing, with Bob accusing Carol of messing around with some other man. This argument was slowing building in volume until all the other customers could not help but notice. Meanwhile, Ted and Carol are trying to soothe things down, to no avail.

Bob is getting louder and angrier, shouting at Carol that he has warned her if she fucked off on him one more time that he was going to blow her ass away. Carol is shouting back at Bob that she didn't give a fuck what he said and that he didn't have guts enough to shoot her, and that it would take a real man with balls to kill someone, and that she would fuck anybody she felt like fucking, whenever and wherever she felt like it.

Now that was the final straw that broke the camel's back. Bob reaches into his jacket pocket where he has the starting pistol concealed, brings out the pistol, waves it about to make sure the audience is well aware that he has a gun (By this stage they well and truly have their audience captured).

Bob shouts, "No guts, you unfaithful bitch, then take this," and fires three shots into Carol at point blank range—the crack of the shots, the muzzle flash, the acrid smell of the gun powder, all adding to the realism of the scene. Carol screams, then moans, and falls back into the arms of one of the local girls they know quite well.

After a moment of stunned silence, a ton of shit hits the fan. You have never seen so many people empty a crowded pub in such a short time. There was a stampede for the doors, the fire escape, and even the windows were thrown open and used as a means of rapid exit. At this point, they realize that they may have overplayed this act just a tiny bit. Bob tells Carol to get up off her ass to show the few people that are still remaining that she is not hurt, to which Carol replied that, "She couldn't." Bob looked to see what she meant only to find their girlfriend holding Carol down telling her "Not to move," crying her eyes out, and reassuring Carol that, "The ambulance was on its way and that she would be all right, just don't move."

And she was right, the ambulance was on the way, along with the police, whom had been called by some conscientious John Q. Citizen.

Well, the only thing that saved Bob, Carol, Ted and Alice's asses, was the bartender who could see that he would lose all the money these assholes spent every week if they went to jail and was able to head the police off with some statement about it all being some misunderstanding on the part of John Q. Citizen.

So, there you have it; Gorilla Theater at its worst. If you still want to try it, all I can say is "God Bess you"—you poor, stupid, foolish asshole. Because you see, Bob, Carol, Ted and Alice retired after their last great performance. As Bob and Ted said afterwards, "diving is a hell of a lot safer."

Soups Up

Another incident of good old Gorilla Theater that comes to mind happened so many years ago that it is now almost ancient history.

Our gorilla actor was a Navy diver named Blacky, and to be absolutely honest, Blacky was really a gorilla in more ways than one. He was big, almost as big as a gorilla. He looked like a gorilla with the back of his hands almost dragging on the ground, he was as hairy as a gorilla, and come to think of it, he was as about as intelligent as a gorilla. As I look back and reread the above sentence, I start to wonder if Blacky ever checked out his family tree. And even in that statement, I couldn't help myself from using the word tree (i.e., swinging from the trees).

I am really being unfair to Blacky. He may have been ugly, he may have been mean, he may even have had a nasty streak, but he was really a nice guy (sic), and his one redeeming quality was that he appreciated the fine arts, for he was a Gorilla Theater performer extraordinary.

Blacky had all the ability required to perform a perfect act. He had a perfect sense of timing that would make the cliff divers of Acapulco green with envy. He also had a perfect touch of the dramatics required to capture his audience without exposing his hand. The one thing he enjoyed above all other things in this world, including drinking beer and chasing pussy, was to shock the poor slobs who were not fortunate enough to be deep sea divers.

The local pub that the frogmen frequented was fairly familiar with some of the more unusual things that these animals were capable of getting up to. But I don't believe they were ready for the performance they were about to experience the day that

Blacky came walking into the frogmen's hang-out, a bar named THE PLANK. He was playing his hand to a tee, pretending to be so drunk that he could hardly stand up, reeling from side to side, staggering, stumbling drunk, making his way to the bar where he ordered a beer. Meanwhile, all the other patrons were watching this act with a great deal of apprehension. Any bartender in the world, except the bartender at the Plank, would have refused to serve any ordinary person that drunk, but since he relied on these fearless frogmen for a large portion of his business, you could see that he figured the best thing to do was go ahead and serve Blacky.

Besides, he had seen him in the same state a number of times in the past. Not only that, after one look at Blacky, nobody in their right mind would consider not serving him, that is if you placed any value on your life and had a desire to continue enjoying some of the finer things in this world, like breathing and living for instance.

Blacky received his beer, looked around the bar reeling from side to side, peering through drunken eyes at the other customers watching him, and he picked up his beer and in one long chug-a-lug drank it in one go. He stood there for a few moments, then began to retch, holding his stomach, with foam running out of his mouth, swaying back and forth. Well, it was very obvious to everyone in that bar he was about to upchuck, in other words spew his guts out. Needless to say, it didn't take long for most of the people in that bar to give Blacky a wide berth. I mean, after all, who wants puke sprayed all over them?

Now that Blacky had the complete and undivided attention of his audience, he went into the climax of his performance. With all the sound effects of his retching and his drunken act of swaying and reeling about, unnoticed he reached into the breast pocket of his jacket. (Where prior to entering the bar, he had carefully placed a can of one of the more famous brands of Chunky meat and vegetable soups). With the loudest retch yet, he bent over the bar so that his audience couldn't see him splash the soup onto the bar top. There were large chunks of carrots, potatoes, peas, and meat running all over the top of the bar.

This would have been a perfect climax to a Gorilla Theater scene, with about half the people in there running for the toilets to spew their guts out, and the other half thinking about what an animal this man was. But Blacky, looked very embarrassed and gave the impression that he was trying to clean up the mess he had just made. Using his hand, he raked and scraped the mess off the bar back into his empty glass. Then, in a state of drunken confusion, he looked around trying to figure out what to do with the glass full of soup/puke. As all of those green-around-the-gills unsuspecting suckers watched, a look of enlightenment came over Blacky's face, and he lifted the glass and, once again, chug-a-lugged it down in one go.

CHAPTER

EIGHT

The Right Stuff

It is a very difficult job indeed to describe what a real diver is; there is a book that was published a couple of years back entitled *THE RIGHT STUFF.* This book (if you haven't already read it, I highly recommend that you do, it's excellent) was all about the United States Space Program, mainly the people, the test pilots, and the astronauts. These were the kind of people that were considered to have the Right Stuff.

In the diving industry, including the Navies, the phrase 'the right stuff' has also been used (At least since I joined the U.S. Navy in 1961) to describe the individual who seems to always make the right decision at the right time—a man who can think on his feet, a man who is flexible enough to bend with the tide, a man strong enough to resist the strongest currents when the necessity arises, a man who is courageous and brave, but modest, in fact, a man who all men, regardless of their own profession, look up to and wish they could emulate, not with envy, but with admiration. Because these are the types of men that make the world go round. These men you will find in all walks of life from the farmers of this world to the leader of our nations.

I feel certain that the phrase—the right stuff—originated in the military services, and has been carried over into civil activities such as the airline pilots and in particular, commercial divers. I am not saying that all divers, be they Navy or commercial, have the 'right stuff' but what I am saying is the diving industry has more than its fair share of the type of men that could be said to have the 'right stuff.' For a man to even select the diving industry as a means of earning his livelihood, he must have some of the traits that go into making up the 'right stuff.'

After you have read this book, you will have the impression that diving is all fun and games. (I have written the book with humor in mind.) But I can assure you that it is not all fun and games. A diver is offshore for one reason and one reason only, and that is to work. His profession requires that he maintain his body in a physical state of fitness so that he is capable of spending as many as eight hours underwater every day in a saturation mode; four hours in the bell tending his fellow diver, and four hours locked out of the bell doing whatever is required of him. The other 16 hours he will spend in the sat chamber (a steel cylinder 7 or 8 feet in diameter and 15 to 20 feet long) preparing his reports, eating, sleeping and waiting for his turn to dive again. Only a few years ago, these periods of saturation exposure were normally for 30 days, and on occasions, men have spent well over 2 months in saturation. If a diver doesn't have the right stuff, these long periods of isolation and hard work will soon expose his weakness.

Diving by its very nature weeds out the men that are unsuitable. If you have any phobias, i.e., fear of the dark, fear of water, fear of death, fear of high places, fear of confined spaces, fear of creepy crawlers, fear of beasts with long sharp teeth, fear of slimy creatures, etc., you won't last long as a diver. The underwater world abounds with all of the unspeakables that most people have nightmares about, and even some that give good divers nightmares. Like jumping into a moon pool in the middle of the night in Indonesia, where there are 16 species of poisonous sea snakes, or mud hole diving in the middle of a swamp, with crocodiles or alligators and poisonous snakes or snapping turtles that can remove one of your fingers in one quick snap. The oceans are full of things that bite, sting, puncture, squeeze, shock, poison, etc.; these various types of marine life will hurt you if you are careless; they will kill you if you are foolish.

That is the environment that you have to work in, and we haven't even mentioned all the other things that you depend on to maintain your life support, or the job that you may be working on. There are hundreds of tons of steel hanging over your head on a thin wire, or equipment can fall over the side to come crashing down on you—all of the thousand and one things that can go wrong, like losing your air or gas supply, becoming fouled on bottom, or even having a ditch or hole cave in, entrapping you, or diving under ice where there is no way to the surface except through the hole that you entered. Or, what happens when you lose your heating in sub-zero temperatures, where your life expectancy becomes measured in seconds, literally a couple of minutes in zero-degree water and you will be dead from exposure. The medical term is hypothermia.

These are only a few of the things that can go wrong that will claim your life, or leave you seriously injured. Every diver faces death at least once in his diving career. The ones who have faced it only once, usually are the ones that retire after the first time it happens. The rest will face death many times, if they continue to pursue diving as a career. There is a saying in the diving industry, "there are young bold divers, but no old bold divers." The point is as plain as the nose on your face, if you are bold or foolish, you are not going to live long enough to be considered old.

We still haven't answered the question, what makes a man decide to become a diver? To risk his life doing things that he is not particularly well paid for doing, spending long periods of time away from his family, considered foolish by 90% of the people he meets, plus all the other factors that you can think of why not to be a diver. If you know the answer, it would be appreciated if you would tell. After all these years, I still don't know. I can only assume it's a combination of the right stuff, foolhardiness, and a quest for danger; after all, it is said, "danger is the spice of life."

I would like to add here, even though I have been downright unfair to diver's women in this book, their women are just as important as the divers. They also have 'the right stuff', otherwise they wouldn't be around. They (the majority) support their men with all their hearts.

Just try criticizing their men and see what happens. You will definitely have a tiger by the tail.

I haven't broached the subject of women divers because in the offshore diving industry, women still haven't made any noticeable impact, but times are changing and there is now beginning to be an interest shown by women.

That's not to say there are no women involved in diving. There have been a great many women involved for years in scientific research, such as oceanography, marine biology, and nature documentaries, etc.

If I have offended the women's liberation movement, please accept my humble apology. I must have a fixation about women, it's a subject that keeps cropping up. As men say, "you can't live with them and you can't live without them."

Like I said before, "They have got the right stuff."

Here are a few little tales that depict what I would consider to be the 'right stuff'.

Graham, a rough, tough, North Sea diver was working on a jack-up drilling rig that had been installed with a small bounce diving system. On this particular day, the diving crew were performing general maintenance to the system. Graham was not only a good diver but was also a damn good mechanic and had decided that he would check out and lubricate the sheave on the tip of the bell launch davit. To make the job easier, he swung the davit over the top of the jack house which was 135 feet above the sea. Graham climbed to the top of the jack house and was in the process of greasing the sheave when another diver on the crew came along and saw that the davit wasn't in its right position and, not realizing that Graham was working on it, swung the davit outboard to reposition it where it belonged. Some of the other crew members saw what was happening, but before they could stop the swinging of the davit, or warn Graham, he was pushed off the top of the jack house falling 135 feet into a sea so cold it would freeze the balls off that brass monkey everyone always refers to. Now this is where the right stuff comes in. Graham, while falling 135 feet, did a double gainer, hit the sea with barely a splash (a perfect score of 10), popped to the surface, swam to the jack-up's leg, climbed the 120 feet back to the main deck of the rig without a pause, and made his way back to the diving system location where the crew were preparing to prevent Graham from doing bodily harm to his fellow crew member.

To the relief of everyone, Graham just looked at his mate and said, "Hell, forget it, everyone makes a mistake now and again." Shook hands with his mate and went to put on dry clothes.

When Graham returned, he was asked why he had executed the dive while he was falling? To which Graham replied, "if you've got to go, go in style."

Graham's attitude about the whole ordeal is what the 'right stuff' is all about.

There are other ways for a man to show that he has the 'right stuff' other than being brave or smart or being a leader or any other way you can think of. Here is a little tale of how the 'right stuff' can show up in the most unusual circumstances.

There was a diver who was planning to marry the girl of his dreams (so his girl said). As the big day drew closer, his diving buddies made plans to give him a stag party that he would never forget. It would be a night of fun and revel, lots of booze, plenty of women (the two most important things that a diver thinks about when he is ashore). It would be a night of hell-raising that would be the talk of the town.

The big night arrived, and the lads set off to one of the nice hotels in town which they proceeded to take over. They ran all the locals out of the hotel with their outrageous performances. There were so many of them, they were stacked six deep at the bar. If you were claustrophobic, you didn't stand a chance. This night got so out of hand that the next day the hotel had to have the carpets in the bar replaced before they could open for business.

The hotel staff did finally manage to get these slightly (sic) drunk party makers out of the hotel only two hours after official closing time. Arrangements by this time had been made to move on to another diver's flat. As they piled out of the hotel, I understand it was very unsafe to be on the streets for the next hour or so until all those gentlemen arrived at the next party.

All the groom's mates had gotten together and arranged for Slack Alice to entertain the groom on his last night as a bachelor and free man, just so that he would realize all the joys that he would be missing from now on. But would you believe that the groom became so inebriated that he was unable to partake of the charming affection that Alice was willing to bestow. One of the groom's best friends, who just happened to be already married and being such a good friend, agreed to fill in for the groom so as Slack Alice wouldn't be put out.

Late the next day, very late the next day indeed, before the hangover had completely disappeared the groom's mates called him and the bride-to-be, and said they were all meeting at a hotel (you are right, a different hotel) for one last night of celebration before the big day. Well, the bride and groom-to-be arrived and you would have thought the party was still going on from the night before, and for a number of the partiers it was still the same party. Divers do have a tendency to carry things like partying to extremes.

As the evening wore on, the groom found himself sitting in a booth with his mate who had filled in for him with Slack Alice the night before and sitting in between him and his mate was his mate's wife. She does not look exactly pleased as it seems that her husband arrived home early that morning with a large love bite on his neck, and when she asked where in the hell, he had gotten a love bite (as if she didn't know), he came up with some cock and bull story about the groom giving it to him the night before. She believed that like she still believed in Santa Claus and the tooth fairy.

Here she now sat, with that, 'I have got you now, you son of a bitch' look in her eyes. She, knowing that she has her husband by the balls, asked the groom if he gave her husband a love bite. The groom may have lost a lot of his gray matter in the last few days but he still was not born yesterday and twigged as to what was coming down. He denied that he would do a thing like that. After all, did she think he was some kind of fruit or a faggot. All this time, he was enjoying the sick expression on his mate's face, and the look of triumph on his wife's face.

Then with absolutely perfect timing, a split second before the shit hits the fan, he dived across his mate's wife's lap, grabbed his mate and threw a lip lock on his neck that would have caused a love bite on Superman's neck.

Now, that is what I would call a perfect example of the right stuff. He got his own back on his mate, and at the same time bailed him out of the shit, or should I say, saved his ass?

Second Thoughts

Here is another quick example of the 'right stuff.'

Standing in a bar one day, our fearless diver is talking and having a good time with one of his old mates who just happens to be so big they usually call him the 'Jolly Green Giant.'

When, as frequently happens, in these joints of little light and lots of alcoholic refreshments, it's not long before someone consumes enough 'Dutch courage' to decide that he is the meanest, toughest, most courageous son of a bitch in the world. He is going to kick ass and take names; he is absolutely sure that he can kick the shit out of the biggest man in the bar. So, here are four or five young men full of piss and vinegar, egging on their "Captain Courageous" to go ahead and have a go at the Jolly Green Giant.

Our fearless diving friend, watching Captain Courageous' friends trying to incite him to have a go at the Giant, picks out the ringleader, the most boisterous of the agitators, and approaches him with a coin in his hand, which he offers to the agitator by saying, "Here is Ten Pence for you" to which the ringleader belligerently enquires, "What the hell is this for?" Our fearless hero replies, "For you to go call an ambulance, because you are going to need one when the Jolly Green Giant tears your head off and shits inside it."

Needless to say, it didn't take the ringleader long to decide that after further consideration, fighting was not the best form of entertainment the evening had to offer, and it seemed like a good time to move to some other part of town. This particular pub was looking decidedly hazardous to his health.

The above was a perfect way to defuse a nasty situation and our hero made the ideal decision, in other words he had the 'right stuff.'

CHAPTER
NINE

Potpourri

In this chapter, I have decided to include the things that I would like to tell, but don't really know where they slot into the other diving stories; they will not necessarily have a relation with diving. That's why I have decided to call this chapter "POTPOURRI." Not only that, but potpourri is also an applicable term for a diver, he is definitely a mixture, a mixture of good and bad. My good old twentieth century dictionary gives the following definitions. "Mixed stew, a mixture of sweet-scented materials, chiefly dried petals, from *pourri,* meaning rotten." That must apply to divers, at least the rotten part, but I must admit I can't possibly think of any diver I ever met, whom you would think of calling petal. The thesaurus certainly does have a number of definitions that I think apply to divers. Here are a few of the uses of potpourri: "Mixture, mingling, harmonization, union, insertion, interlarding, interweaving, interlacing, crossing, amalgamation, fusion, infusion, impregnation, adulteration, cross-fertilization, hybridism, hybridization, mixer, melting pot, etc. etc."

And so it goes—on and on. I feel that some, if not all those terms apply to divers in some form or fashion. (PLEASE NOTE: some of these definitions are completely beyond my comprehension. After all, dumb ass divers are not expected to know everything. So, you will have to take the time to look up the definitions of these words for yourselves).

Take "Mixture"—a diver is a mixture of a little good and a lot of bad. Take "mingling," there is nothing that a diver would rather do than mingle, especially with the opposite sex . . . Then there is "Union", a diver always believes in a union, between man and women. Impregnation?

Do I really need to comment on that one? Adulteration? He expects nothing less, insertion really! If you just look at the other definitions, I am sure you can come up with how a diver will fit them all in some way, so though I have not covered them all you can see a diver is absolutely a potpourri.

A Diver's Sixth Sense

A story that an old abalone diver, named Dick, once told me, about the time he was diving off the Channel Islands in California, is enough to make you think twice about going diving.

Before I get into the story, here is a little background and history on the abalone diving industry in California. What a lot of people don't know is just how important a role that some of these abalone divers played in the offshore commercial diving industry. Many of them pioneered the first use of helium gas diving for the oil industry, this was in the late Fifties and early Sixties, just when offshore exploration was moving into what in those days was deep water, 250 to 350 feet.

If you were not part of this "clique", you didn't get any deep gas work from the oil companies. There are some of those old abalone divers still around to this day, and some of you divers are still working for them, for there are several large diving companies that these men are still running or own or are part owners (Before you say what a dumb ass I am, try checking this fact out, you may find yourselves in for a surprise).

You should be getting used to me running off onto different tangents by now, as I've said before "I digress," so back to the abalone business. There are four main types of abalone in Californian waters that the divers were picking (Note: that word picking—I will come back to it later with a little tale). I don't know how the abalone business is today, but fourteen years ago it was a dying industry. The abalone had been overexploited to the point that they were no longer a profitable business in the early Seventies.

Anyway, in the good old days, when a diver could make a living diving ABS. There were the four types, the Black Ab, found in very shallow water, these would be exposed clinging to the rocks in the splash zone at low tide.

These abalone had almost no commercial value. The next least valuable Abs were the Greens. These would be found in slightly deeper water, clinging to the rocks in the kelp beds, in water depths from around 20 to 40 feet. And, as I have said, these had very little commercial value at the period I am describing, the mid-sixties. Now we begin to get into the abalones that were of commercial value; the next abalone you would come across as you progressed into deeper water was the pink abalone. These would be found just on the outer fringe of the kelp beds, in water depths ranging from 50 to 80 feet. These were the abalone diver's main source of income, giving best value for the bottom time that the divers could spend at these depths.

But the most valuable abalone were found in even deeper water; these were the giant red abalone and were found in water depths ranging from around 70 feet down to 100 feet or more. These were the abalone that the packers most preferred as they were the finest eating shellfish in the world (that's my opinion)— large, snow-white abalone steaks, fit for a king. Mussels, clams, scallops, etc. can't hold a candle to the abalone when it comes to the flavor and texture of one of those steaks.

The grounds for abalone diving were from San Diego to just north of Moro Bay. North of this, the abalone are protected by the state. The prime abalone grounds were off the coast near Santa Barbara. Here were located the Channel Islands where some of the most beautiful diving on the California coast was to be found. So, there was quite a large abalone diving industry working out of Santa Barbara, one of the most beautiful small cities on the West Coast.

Any day of the week, you could go to Sterns Wharf and observe the abalone boats either coming in with a load or just departing for two or three days, to dive for this much sought-after shellfish. The boats were small, usually no more than thirty feet long, with very powerful engines capable of powering these boats to speeds of between 20 and 30 knots. The name of the game was speed. It required a fast boat to make a quick run out to the Islands where the divers would spend a day or two diving until they had a full load. Then there was a quick trip (and here was where those fast boats came into their own, for it was not unusual to find yourself in a race with another AB boat to get to the packer first because he who arrived first got the best price for his load) into Santa Barbara where they would unload, refuel, stock the refrigerator with a fresh supply of steaks, and a few more gallon jugs of Red Mountain wine and then another quick dash across the Channel to get another load of abalone before the next boat beat them to a good diving area. These boats were usually privately owned, and only had a crew of two, very seldom more than three, and in most cases, all the crew members were divers.

These boats consisted of little more than a small cabin, a tank that sea water could be circulated through to stow the ABS, and engines, with a small area set aside for a small diving compressor.

By law, all commercial abalone diving had to be conducted using surface supplied air, i.e., no scuba diving permitted.

So, all the diving was done using the live boat technique, i.e., the boat's engine was used to maneuver the boat, and follow the diver wherever he went. This is not the safest way to dive in the best of circumstances, and when you are trying to follow a diver in a kelp bed with currents, tides and winds causing the boat to drift, and the diver's umbilical becomes entangled in the kelp, rocks and etc., it was not uncommon for these divers to have serious accidents. But these divers loved this life, and wouldn't have done anything else, for this was one of those type of jobs that not very many people ever have a chance to experience in a lifetime. You were your own boss. You came and went as you pleased, and even the hard work, the diving, was that supreme of all topics, FUN, FUN, FUN. What can be more rewarding than performing a job that you really enjoy?

I feel that these guys really deserve a place in the history of diving, along with the old sponge divers and I guess even the coral divers. I suppose there are others that also deserve a mention but since I am not familiar with those, I will leave that subject to someone who is more "clued in" than me.

Back to the "Old Abalone Diver." Dick tells the story of how he was diving just on the fringe of a kelp bed out at the Channel Islands one day. He describes the day as one of those days that are so beautiful, it makes you appreciate being alive just to witness this one day. At the Islands this day, the weather was absolutely perfect, the temperature in the low eighties, the wind blowing less than 5 knots, the sun sparkling and shining off of a smooth flat calm ocean, and the seas and swell almost non-existent. A perfect early summer day.

Dick goes on to describe how he was working a reef in about 60 feet of water, really enjoying himself. The bottom was rock, with large cracks and crevasses with a fair amount of kelp growing up to the surface, but not thick enough to cause him any problems with his umbilical or the boat any difficulties tracking him. The sunshine was glittering and bouncing down from the surface, constantly moving and flickering from the movement of the kelp gently swaying in the slight surge, causing a dancing dappled effect on the ocean bottom.

So, here he was having a good day, finding plenty of abalone. He had already sent up to the surface enough ABS for half a boat load, when that sense that we have discussed earlier came into play. The one we call the sixth sense, where the hairs on the back of your neck stand up, and a cold chill runs down (or up, please yourselves) your spine, your hands and lips tremble and you know there is a very good (or bad, depending on your point of view) possibility that you may be in the shit.

Dick goes on to say that at about this time, a large shadow begins to pass over him and he knows that it is not the boat because he can see the bottom of the boat up above and off to the side of him. As he turns around to see what is causing this large shadow, he sees a giant basking shark. (The basking shark is one of the biggest sharks in the oceans, the only sharks that get bigger are the great white shark, and the whale shark. The basking shark is not normally considered a dangerous shark, but they get so big that you don't want to fool around with them anyway; it is not unusual for these sharks to exceed 20 feet).

Dick says that when he turned around and saw this huge shark it definitely gave him a fright for a moment, but as soon as he realized that it was a basking shark, he was not overly concerned but he still thought it would be prudent not to expose any more of himself than absolutely necessary. He backed up to a large rock that he was close by at the time, while keeping an eye on the shark overhead, and that is when Dick, as he said in his own words, "Shit my drawers, because the rock swam away."

It was a giant grouper that Dick had decided to use as a refuge and hadn't realized that it was there at the time because all his attention was focused on the basking shark.

These giant groupers can get huge; they will grow to five or six hundred pounds, even as much as 1,000 pounds.

These giants are usually what you would classify as gentle giants. Divers who have been around them, tell how they are just curious; when you are working, they will come around you and get in the way trying to see what you are doing, but never harm you. Divers even give these giants names, because they are very territorial; if they take up habitats around one of the offshore structures, they always remain in the near vicinity.

There is one story that has been floating around the diving industry for years about groupers that for some reasons were not gentle giants. These were the bad guys on the block (I guess). In the Gulf of Mexico there were a group of groupers (a little pun) that kept terrifying the divers who were diving on an offshore structure, and the one story that sticks out in my mind is of a diver being harassed by one of the groupers, to the point that the diver was trying to fight him off and make his way back to the bell. When he did reach the bell, while trying to scramble into the hatch, the grouper took his foot into his mouth up to the knee, and with the diver's struggles and the efforts of the bell tender pulling as hard as he could to get the diver into the bell, the grouper actually pulled the diver's diving boot off. At the time, I found it hard to believe that these groupers were being aggressive, but later on I had heard that these divers may have caused this reaction themselves. They had been blasting the creatures with a high-pressure water jet while cleaning the structure. So maybe these creatures were smarter than we would give them credit for. After all, it sounds to me as if they were protecting their territory, and rightly so if those asshole divers were in fact aggravating them.

I may sound like a conservationist by some of the statements I occasionally make, and I guess that in some ways I am, but don't get me wrong, I believe in getting my share of the bugs, abalone, fish, etc., out of the sea (And in many cases more than my share and if I ever come across the giant bug that I have been looking for half my life down there, he is in a world of shit because I am going to do everything in my power to get his ass into the pot. But his shell will go with pride into my trophy collection). I don't believe in killing or harassing the sea creatures just for the sheer hell of it.

Divers love fast cars; they also love drinking enormous quantities of booze and, as your local police like to stress, fast cars and booze are not a particularly good combination if you wish to die of old age. It is most unfortunate the number of our diving buddies who have lost their lives in diving accidents, but even more tragic are the numbers we have lost to the automobiles and in many cases whilst driving under the influence of intoxicating drinks such as tequila. No, I am not going to get into that old argument of whether or not it's the lemon first then the salt or is it the salt first then the lemon. Oh, to hell with it. Which brings me to a story on that very subject.

Serious Bullshit

Adrian deep sea diver extraordinaire, who was infamous for his bad driving (Not diving, he was infamous for that as well) and drinking. He had destroyed so many cars that Hertz and Avis girls used to throw rocks at him when he was just passing through the airport, on his way to the bar. The bartender there would welcome him as if he was his long-lost brother so you can see he was fairly well-known for his bad habits. You can imagine the shock that some of his friends exhibited when Adrian bought himself a turbocharged-super-go-fast wopmobile, for they were sure that Adrian would kill himself within a week at the outside.

While Adrian was being ostentatious talking and strutting about his new super car, one of his mates brought Adrian down to earth when he told Adrian that he would give him a whole case of tequila free and purchase an insurance policy for the rest of Adrian's life, if Adrian would make him the beneficiary on the policy. As he said to Adrian, "It'll only cost me a case of tequila and one month's insurance coverage and I will be able to retire from the diving game."

Well, I thought that was pretty funny, but Adrian didn't think it was funny at all; he thought it was damn callous of his mate. But the next week after he had wrapped that TURBO-SUPER-CAR around a tree while driving it so drunk he couldn't hit his ass with both hands and had come away with his life, he finally saw the point that his mate was trying to make and sold his new toy.

That is, what was left of it. At least he is still alive today, thanks to his mate. The moral of this story is that sometimes you should take even bullshit seriously.

The One With The Goat

Speaking of drunk divers and cars this is a little short story about just that subject.

Two very drunk divers were coming home from a job one night after quite a lengthy stay at a pub they had found on their way home. They had spent many enjoyable hours telling each other what great divers they were, and how lucky the company they worked for was, etc. After they had exhausted this subject, one of them happened to mention what a great cook he was, and that there was nothing in this world as good as a goat—assuming you knew how to properly barbeque one, and how to make a barbeque sauce that was out of this world. (You will find, for some reason that I have never been able to figure out, every diver you ever meet thinks he is the best barbeque artist in the world. This is a crock of bullshit. They can't be the best because, you see, there is only one that is the best, and how could they be that one, seeing as how I am the best barbequer this world has ever seen and probably ever will see). Well, seeing as how this subject of barbequing was on their minds, on the way home on a back road, what should show up alongside the road in their headlights but a goat. Well, this seemed like an ideal time to acquire a goat to demonstrate their superior barbequing skills.

Without a word being spoken between them, they knew what to do. The driver slammed on the brakes while the other diver jumped out of the car and grabbed the goat while his mate opened the trunk/boot. The goat was thrown into the trunk/boot, the lid slammed shut; they scrambled back into the car and with the tires screaming and a cloud of smoke boiling from the rear of the car, they were gone. The snatch had taken mere seconds. They congratulated each other on another job well done, opened a can of beer and had a long slug while contemplating the fine barbeque they would have for all their friends the following day. When suddenly what should appear in the rearview mirror but a flashing light and the sound of a police siren. Being law abiding (sic) citizens, they pulled over and waited for the policeman to come to the window of the car.

The policeman approached the car and very politely said to the driver, "Excuse me, sir, but it looks like you have snagged a chain with a goat attached to it and you are dragging him behind you." Well, the divers didn't quite know what to make of this statement, having expected to get a ticket for speeding. When they replied that they didn't understand what he was talking about, the police officer told them to come along and he would show them. They got out of the car and followed the policeman to the rear of the car were there was indeed a dead goat attached to a chain. Again, the policeman explained they must have hooked the chain somehow on their car, and with his flashlight he followed the chain back to the car to see how they had snagged it, only to see the chain disappear into the trunk/boot of their car. Now looking very suspicious, he asked them to open the trunk/boot, and lo and behold, there attached to the other end of the chain what did he find but one live goat.

Our drunk divers, in their state of slightly pissed, (sic) befuddled minds had not even realized that the goat they had snatched was attached to a chain, let alone staked with another goat on the other end of the chain.

After they got out of jail for rustling, drunk driving, speeding, and a multitude of other crimes that you wouldn't even know existed, they said they, ". . . never wanted to go to another goat barbeque as long as they lived."

If those two happen to read this little story, will they ever be surprised; I am sure they had thought that everybody had forgotten about that little episode eons ago.

Dealer's Choice

Divers, you may be surprised to learn, as a rule are not big gamblers, and by that, I mean games of chance. They gamble with their lives everyday, but when it comes to sitting down at the table and putting their cash on the line, they seem to lose all that nerve that they are so famous, or is it infamous, for. Could it be that they haven't lost their nerve, and are just making sure that they will have plenty of cash to spend on the ladies when they hit the beach?

You did note, I hope, that I said as a rule because the divers that do gamble sure as hell are gamblers. They take their gambling damn seriously, some of them are winners and some are losers just like all gamblers in this world. Some always win and some always lose; some play cautiously, and some play recklessly, some play smart cards and some play dumb cards, and then some play downright stupid cards and should take up tiddlywinks for their amusement.

What all this bullshit brings me to is gambling offshore. On most big construction barges there are a few games of chance of rather small stakes being played after shift change. But these games are more for amusement and something to pass the time than anything else; you could make a few dollars or lose a few, but you were never going to get rich or on the other hand, you were never going to get hurt badly because these little games would have a couple dollars' limit.

The REAL games usually took place on the big pipelay barges where you had a large crew of 300 or 400 men, and then only when the weather got so bad that it shut the job down. Then grab your knickers, because as sure as the sun will rise and set each day, there was going to be a big game of dealer's choice poker.

I should clarify what I mean by big because everybody has their own opinion. Like my old granddaddy used to say, "opinions are like assholes, everybody has one." So, what's small to me may be big to you and vice versa. My idea of big, is a game that runs non-stop for 36 to 48 hours with six or seven players, and each pot has $500-$600 in it. With many pots running to $1,500-$1,800. It is not a game to join if you are faint of heart.

Some of these games would get even bigger; it was not that unusual to see a $5,000 diamond ring in the pot or even a $8,000 gold Rolex. On several occasions, I have seen $20,000 cars put up, but the one that sticks out in my mind, is when one of the hands bet his house, worth $60,000 on a hand of cards. He was called and lost. I guess like they say, "you win some and you lose some."

Once a diver told me he would go offshore and work for nothing if he could go on a lay barge; he said he could make more playing in the poker games than he could diving. That may or may not have been the truth, but I do know for a fact a welder who made over sixty thousand dollars one season playing poker, and that is not exactly chicken feed.

If you ever get offshore and decide that you want to sit down and take a hand, let me advise you now, you had better spend some time learning the games. As I mentioned, it is dealer's choice and that means when it's your deal, you deal any game of your choice. I can tell you there are some wild, weird, and wonderful poker games e.g., High-Low Split Shuck Two, Ace In The Hole, Texas Rip-Ass, Baseball, Hold 'em—Fuck 'em, Doctor Pepper, Holy-Cross, just to name a few. Then, of course, there are the ones that you all know, like 5 and 7 Card Stud, and Draw Poker. Like I said, don't sit down until you learn the rules, because if you don't, you are going to get your ass ripped.

In these games, you will find a few divers but not many. However, you will find them betting on some of the weirdest things you can imagine: for instance, which drop of water on a windowpane will reach the bottom first; will the left wheel on an airplane touch down before the right; or even will their mate score with that lady he has been chasing.

All I can say about divers and gambling is that they are weird, gambling with their lives, but not their money.

I made a point in Chapter Five of this book that the divers of today are not like the divers of only a few years ago, and by that, I mean that there is not the same sense of urgency when it comes to getting into the water and getting a job done. The deep-sea divers who consider themselves the '*numero uno*' divers of this era, the saturation divers, have been spoiled, and there is no other word for their attitude. They have become a bunch of *prima donnas*. Maybe you think I don't know what I am talking about, but after 20 odd years in this business, I feel I just may have an idea of what the hell goes on. I have spent since 1961 involved in the diving industry in some form or fashion, beginning as a Navy diver, and after I was discharged from the U.S. Navy in 1966, I went to work in the commercial diving field, beginning as a diving tender working my way up through the ranks. For the last 8 years, I have been working as the diving manager in the North Sea for one of the largest construction companies in the world. If in your opinion, that doesn't qualify me to comment on the standards of divers in the commercial diving industry, I suggest that you throw this book into the trash (no cash refunds) and forget everything you have read up to now. Because I still have a few things to say regarding the quality of the divers employed in the North Sea today.

Before I continue, I offer my apologies to those good divers, who have been offended by the above statement; they know who they are. As for the rest of you wankers, you know who you are as well. All I have to say is, tough shit.

A Little Rant

I will start this with the example I used in Chapter Five where a diver used to be standing on the bottom hatch so that when the pressure equalized, the bottom hatch of the bell opened and he merely dropped out into the water and was on his way to the job site. Time was of the utmost essence. In those deep bounce dives, you were on a very restricted bottom time, and every second counted; nowadays you have some of these saturation divers extraordinaire, who take three quarters of an hour to get locked out of the bell, with the bell on bottom and the bottom hatch open. In the good old days, that was all the time we had to do the complete job.

Why does it take these divers (sic) so long to exit the bell? It is very simple. In the first place, they don't want to lock out—they make the same money sitting on their asses in the sat complex as they do working on the bottom, and it is a hell of a lot easier sitting on your ass reading a book, than it is busting your ass working on bottom.

So, when you do finally get them into the bell and on their way to the bottom, these *prima donnas* don't give a shit whether they get onto the job site to work or not.

They will find every excuse you can think of to avoid locking out into that cold, dark, hostile ocean. Their first and most popular excuse is that the hot water used to heat their suits is too hot or too cold because they know this will take ten to twenty minutes to check out to ascertain that, in fact, it is functioning correctly.

That is just one of the many little ploys they use; there are dozens including, "I just broke my fin strap and there are no spares" (that's because he just dropped the spares out of the hatch), and "My light won't work." In fact, the list is endless. I know the diving supervisors, and diving superintendents who have been around for a while have heard some that are out of this world.

The point I am making about these *prima donnas* being spoiled starts to become apparent when you realize that they don't understand that speed is of paramount importance offshore. Time is money, and you would be surprised how many of these dumb asses think that the longer it takes to do a job, the more money they will make. (This is known as sand-bagging a job.) In actual fact, if they would get on with the job, they will in the long run make more money because a good diver who is making an effort to get the job done will be requested by the client for his next job, and at the end of the day, a diver's reputation is everything.

If some of you *prima donna* deep sea divers extraordinaire who are sitting on the beach, wondering why you can't get a job, try

Working on Sealab. Would have been taken in either Key West (Florida) or La Jolla (California). Using MK 9 gear.

putting a little more effort into it. The next time you get a job (IF YOU EVER GET ANOTHER JOB), you will most likely find that my advice will pay off in the long run.

In Chapter One, I mentioned that while I was in the U.S. Navy, I had worked with a famous porpoise named Tuffy. Tuffy received his name due to the number of scars on his body. One of the scars on his side was a double crescent about fourteen inches across where he had been attacked and bitten by a shark. If the appearance of the scar was anything to go by, he was very lucky to have survived that encounter. As a matter of fact, any creature that survived the number of battles he had obviously been in would have had to be very tough. Thus, Tuffy was the well-earned name that he was given.

The Navy was training Tuffy to assist divers employed in underwater tasks. As this was still fairly experimental work in the mid-sixties, the tasks were of a simple nature, mainly fetching and carrying of tools or messages from the surface to the divers, or between the divers working on bottom.

Tuffy wore a harness with clips and pouches that the tools could be attached to, and an underwater slate for writing messages on. The divers wore on their wrists an underwater acoustic signaling device so that they could send signals calling Tuffy or sending him to the surface or to another diver.

Unfortunately, I never had an opportunity to work with Tuffy as long as I would have liked. But the time I did work with him will always have a fond spot in my heart. I was lucky enough to turn on the television by chance several years ago in time to catch part of a documentary on the use of dolphins, killer whales, pilot whales and porpoises performing various tasks in the underwater world. What pleasure it gave me to see my old friend, Tuffy, with a starring role.

Photo above shows the actual Sealab. The photo below, shows us working on Seal Lab (yours truly is behind the diver in front), again, either Key West or La Jolla. Originally MK6 gear but now MK9. Augmented with additional tanks (nitrogen and helium in big tanks, oxygen in small tank).

During the one week, and three dives I was lucky enough to spend with Tuffy, it made me really appreciate what marvelous creatures these porpoises are. The sheer amount of power they generate with their tails is almost unbelievable; the speeds they are capable of reaching underwater in short distances are unreal. This speed and power gives them the characteristic of appearing and disappearing as if by magic.

The reason that we only had one week to work with Tuffy is that this took place during the U.S. Navy's Man-in-the-Sea Project, Sealab II. Tuffy had been working in the open ocean prior to this time, but previously it had been done with his trainers, people with whom he was familiar and always in controlled situations. It was decided that Tuffy was to be given a chance to show his stuff working in the open ocean with total strangers. Needless to say, there were some very nervous and apprehensive trainers the first time they released him. I am sure they were imagining many months of diligence and patient teamwork swimming off into the sunset. But Tuffy was a gentleman and behaved himself perfectly, never giving one moment of fright to his trainers, which is more than I can say for myself.

That moment of fright came on my very first dive with Tuffy. Another diver and me were sent down to the bottom in about 80 feet of water to put Tuffy through his paces. The plan called for us to stretch a 100-foot line between us and then Tuffy would be called from the surface by the first diver. Subsequently, I was to call him to me along the line that we had stretched between us. The visibility was not great, but not bad either, about 35 feet of murky, milky vis. The first diver signaled me that I should call Tuffy with a tug on the taut line. I turned on the acoustic signaler and peered down the line waiting for Tuffy to approach and like a shot out of the dark there was an inky black, sinister torpedo shooting straight down the taut line at what appeared to be hundreds of knots, hell bent on a collision with me. There wasn't even time to crap my drawers before Tuffy came to a complete stop by standing vertically on his tail and sliding to a dead stop, gently lowering his body and placing his nose on my outstretched wrist. This was how he had been trained, in order that you had easy access to his harness. Well, after I got my heart out of my mouth and had accomplished what I was supposed to do, I gave Tuffy a small piece of fish as a reward and signaled his return to the surface. I watched him disappear with one mighty flip of his tail, and I can tell you that I was mighty impressed, and from then on, I was hooked. What great joy it was to watch this sea creature performing with such grace and skill. What a wonderful feeling to touch Tuffy and to stroke his silky-smooth skin, and to witness his undoubtedly high intelligence. That one week ended all too soon, and now you know why I think the porpoises are intelligent creatures and why I have so much respect for them.

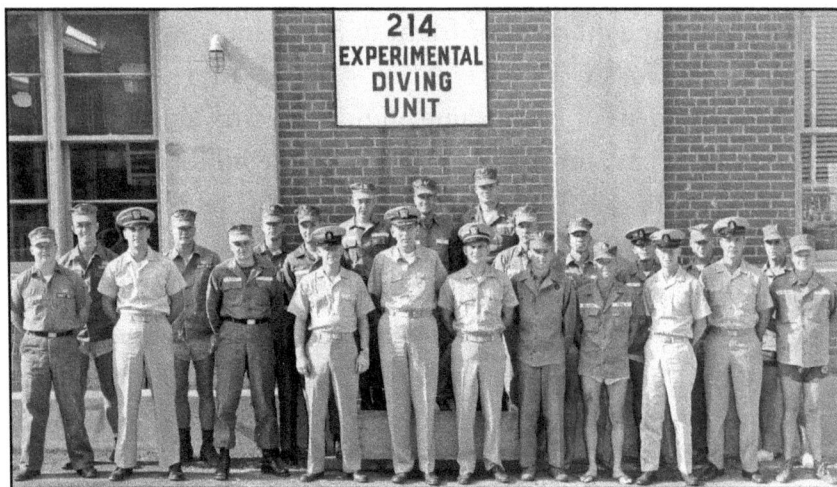

The men selected for Sealab II. Author, Bill Ray Ledford, is in the far back row (3 people), far right.

THE SECRETARY OF THE NAVY
WASHINGTON

The Secretary of the Navy takes pleasure in commending

SEALAB II EXPERIMENTAL UNIT

for service as set forth in the following

CITATION:

For exceptionally meritorious service during Project SEALAB II from 15 August to 15 October 1965. Living at a depth of 205 feet beneath the surface of the Pacific Ocean within a pressure field equal to seven times that of the normal surface pressure, the members of SEALAB II EXPERIMENTAL UNIT successfully completed all assigned tasks, cheerfully and willingly exposing themselves to a hostile and unknown environment to further the capability of the United States Navy in maintaining its position as the leader in the field of undersea rescue and salvage. Their skill, courage, and devotion to duty were in keeping with the highest traditions of the United States Naval Service.

All personnel attached to and serving with Project SEALAB II Experimental Unit during the above period, or any part thereof, are hereby authorized to wear the Navy Unit Commendation Ribbon.

Paul H. Nitze
Secretary of the Navy

HEADQUARTERS, ELEVENTH NAVAL DISTRICT
NAVAL COMMUNICATION STATION, SAN DIEGO

TOR: GGA813CLB190
RR RUWDC
DE RUECW 934 2821727
ZNR UUUUU
R 091727Z
FM SECNAV
TO RUWDC/COMELEVEN
INFO RUWSCU/SCRIPTS INSTITUTE OF OCEANOGRAPHY
RUEPGS/SECRETARY OF THE INTERIOR
RUECD/BUREAU OF COMMERCIAL FISHERIES
RUECM/BUREAU OF MINES
BT
UNCLAS
PLEASE PASS TO SEALAB II. QUOTE: THANKS TO THE TEAMWORK AND DEDICATED
EFFORTS OF THE SCIENTIFIC COMMUNITY, AQUANAUTS AND SUPPORT PERSONNEL,
SEALAB II HAS ACCOMPLISHED ITS MISSION. YOU HAVE PROVED THAT MAN CAN
LIVE AND DO USEFUL WORK UNDER THE SEA. YOUR ACCOMPLISHMENTS DURING THE
PAST 45 DAYS HAVE SET ONE OF THE CORNERSTONES FOR OUR FUTURE EXPLOI-
TATIONOF THE CONTINENTAL SHELF. ADMIRAL MCDONALD JOINS ME IN EXTENDING
TO ALLHANDS OUR SINCERE BEST WISHES AND THE OFFICIAL CONGRATULATIONS
OF THE NAVY DEPARTMENT FOR A JOB WELL DONE! PAUL H. NITZE, SECRETARY
OF THE NAVY UNQUOTE
BT

CNB-2014Z

OO COMDT	02 ACOS ADM	03 ACOS OPR/LOG	34 DCO	AMCROSS	NAVCOMMSTA	
OA CDS	21 ADMIN	03A PLANS	351 MATL	NAVREL	34A	345A
08 DCOS	22 LEGAL	030 MARCOR	352 SECTY/ORD	FSPO	34D	345B
OC AID	23 NAVPERS	31 OPERATIONS	36 MED	TRAAIDS	34E	345C
OO PIO	230 HOUSING	312 DIS. CONT.	37 DENTAL	SHOPAT	34F	346
OE CHAP	234 DISCIPLINE	314 PORTSERV		FWSG	34R	346D
OF INTELL	235 DPTO	315 NCSO/MSTS		PRNRTC		346E
OG IG	236 SPEC. SERV.	32 CIV. ENG.	PUB CLERK	NAAO	341	347
O6 ACOS RESTRA	24 CIVPERS	33 SUPPLY	MAIL ROOM	NRFC	342	348
COMDT MAIL	25 MGT. AST.	3LΦ	TRIBBED	DIO	343	
	27 COMPT				345	

CLE

"A" - ACTION   "COG" - COGNIZANCE   "X" - INFO

TLD:

DTG: 0917 27Z OCT 65

INCOMING MESSAGE   IIND-NCS-2100/7 (REV. 9-65)

DEPARTMENT OF THE NAVY
OFFICE OF NAVAL RESEARCH
WASHINGTON, D. C. 20360

IN REPLY REFER TO

SPECIAL PROJECT
SEALAB II
12 OCTOBER 1965

From: On Scene Commander, Project SEALAB II, Scripps Institution of
Oceanography, La Jolla, California

To: LEDFORD, B. R., EN2, USN

Subj: Navy Unit Commendation Ribbon; presentation of

Encl: (1) Secretary of the Navy Citation - SEALAB II
(2) Navy Unit Commendation Ribbon

1. Enclosures (1) and (2) are presented with pleasure.

2. I wish to add the thanks of the Chief of Naval Research and
the Director, Special Projects Office, in addition to my personal
appreciation to that of the Secretary. Your full cooperation and
hard work, contributed materially to the successful prosecution
of SEALAB II.

RAY C. SPENSER
Captain, U.S. Navy

Sealab II stand-by divers and crew—taken in California. Author, Billy Ray Ledford, is in the back row second from the left.

DIVING EQUIPMENT

One thing that has not been mentioned is the equipment that divers use. So, with that in mind, below is a list of what I consider to be the basic Self-Contained Underwater Breathing Apparatus (SCUBA) equipment:

Face mask: Masks come in all different shapes, sizes and with different features. But we will just focus on the basic mask. The face mask's primary job is to protect the diver's eyes and nose from the water. Its secondary function is to provide maximum visibility. It achieves this by putting a layer of air between the lens of the eye and the water, permitting the diver to focus. This feature is minor in comparison to the psychological value the diver gets by having their eyes and nose protected whilst in the water. For a face mask to function correctly, it has to fit. To ensure a properly fitting mask, the diver holds the mask in place and inhales gently via the nose and lets go. The mask should stay in place solely on suction. The second step in testing the fit is to wear the mask as if the diver was in the water, making sure the straps are adjusted correctly. Again, inhale gently through the nose and the mask should seal. If that happens then the mask fits and should provide a good seal whilst in the water.

Knife: The diving knife is one of the most important tools a diver can have. There are several designs available. The more traditional knife is sharp on one edge and saw toothed on the other. The diving knife should have a corrosion resistant blade, like stainless steel. The hilt or handle should be made of plastic or hard rubber. The knife should be in a protective sheath called a scabbard and should be carried on the diver's calf, hip, or thigh. This is really a personal preference, as long as it does not interfere with the divers movement whilst working or swimming. The scabbard should hold the knife with a positive but easily released lock.

Depth gauge: This item does what is says on the tin— measures the depth of the diver. It achieves this by measuring the pressure of the water above the diver. The depth gauge should be designed to be easily read in limited visibility.

Diver's watch: The divers watch must be waterproof, pressure-proof and equipped with a rotating bezel. It is also necessary that the dial be large and luminous as these aid the diver in reading the watch. The rotating bezel allows the diver to set the dial to indicate elapsed dive time. It is recommended that the watch and depth gauge be worn on the same wrist as they are so closely related to the depth/times consideration of the dive.

Fins: The main purpose of fins is to increase the diver's efficiency in the water. Fins make divers swim faster and further whilst lowering their energy consumption. Like most things, fins come in a variety of different materials and styles. When in the Navy, we focused on two types—straight or offset blades. Both worked well, but the straight blades tended to bring on cramps sooner due to the greater extension of the foot. What makes a good fin? Flexibility? Blade size?

Configuration? Well, each one contributed in different ways. A larger blade typically transmits more power from the leg to the water, allowing the diver to swim faster. But the downside to long fins, is the diver needs to be strong enough to use them. There is no one fin that fits all. As the diver gains experience and strength, they will likely need to change the type of fin used.

Life vest/preserver: In the Navy, a life preserver was a mandatory piece of equipment for scuba operations. Its primary function is to assist a diver in returning to the surface and to help maintain them once there in a head up position. The automatic inflation device is activated by tugging on a cord. This can be activated by the diver or the dive buddy in case of emergency. We used two types: The UDT life preserver and the MK3 yoke type. The UDT was used in surface swimming and to depths of about 36 feet. The MK3 was required for all other types of diving. Both types had a breath tube and automatic inflation systems. The automatic inflation systems used C02 cannisters. The UDT used one 18G CO_2 canister and the Yoke used two 31G canisters.

Scuba tanks: The lifeline of the diver. This along with a regulator allows the diver to breathe whilst underwater. You have three basic types of SCUBA: Open circuit, closed circuit and semi-closed circuit. Open circuit is the only system that is normally used with compressed air as the breathing medium. The other two are designed to be used with a mixture of gases other than air.

A basic set up would be a SCUBA tank connected to the first-stage regulator, connected via a supply hose to the second-stage regulator/mouthpiece. Tanks come in different sizes and materials, EG 72" steel and 90" aluminum. An open circuit 72" steel tank has an internal volume of 700 inches, the air capacity at 62.4 feet is 1767 liters. A 90" aluminum tank at 81.3 feet also has an internal volume of 700 inches and an air capacity of 2353 liters.

Protective clothing: Gloves are primarily designed to protect the divers hands from cuts and chaffing. These can be made from several different materials including rubber, cloth, or leather. They offer little protection from the cold, as thicker gloves limit the use of the divers hands. The rest of the body is protected by either a wet suit or dry suit.

A **wet suit** is normally made of neoprene and comes in different thicknesses, 1/8, 3/16, 1/4 all the way up to 1/2 inch. The thicker the suit the better the insulation but the more restrictive to movement. The wet suit works by allowing a small amount of water to sit between the skin and the inner layer of the suit. The water is then warmed by the heat of the divers body. A properly fitting wet suit must not be so tight that it is uncomfortable or restrictive. The performance of the suit depends on many factors such as, thickness, water temperature and depth. You will find that divers have several suits.

Dry Suit: The dry suit again is made up of closed-cell neoprene, but the main difference is that it is watertight; it does not allow any water between the skin and inner layer. To keep warm, divers wear one or more layers of undergarments of a thermal nature. The dry suit does not fit the same way as the wet suit. Instead of being a snug fit, it is actually a little loose.

Last but not least, what I consider to be the holy grail of diving equipment is the divers' **dive/decompression table**. Without this, it is almost impossible to dive safely at depth for any length of time. Dive tables serve as a guide for divers to know how long they can stay under at a particular depth, how long surface intervals should be, and at what depth. All so they can avoid the life threatening bends.

These items are not always needed but depending upon the requirements of the dive operation, they may become necessary:

Slate and pencil: A basic device used to communicate and/or record data underwater. This item normally made of acrylic due to the high strength and rigidity it offers. The pencil would typically be a regular graphite or a grease pencil.

Wrist Compass: The wrist compass is an aid used for underwater navigation. Not the most precise instrument, it can be worth its weight in gold in low visibility. The compass is normally worn on the opposite wrist from the depth gauge and the watch away from anything magnetic that could interfere with its operation.

Signal Flares: A signal flare is typically used to attract attention. For example, a diver may use the flare whilst on the surface to attract the attention of the boat crew, if he surfaced too far away.

Flashlight: This is an obvious one—needed in low visibility or deep water. The flashlight can be mounted to the divers helmet or around the wrist. It is a good idea to make sure that the flashlight has a lanyard as you don't want to drop it, only for it to disappear into the eerie depths.

Lines: Lines can literally be the lifeline of a diver. This should be used to keep track of diver and to send signals. Used in low visibility when buddy divers are not able to keep track of each other.

There a three basic types of lifelines: Buddy line, surface line and float line. The buddy line is a 6 to 10-foot-long Nylon cable, that attaches to each diver. The surface line is connected to the diver and boat crew, normally used when one diver is working without a buddy diver. And lastly, the float line is attached to the diver and a flotation device on the surface, used primarily for tracking location.

Snorkel: A snorkel is a simple breathing tube that allows the diver to swim on the surface with his face in the water. This is primarily used when working in shallow depths, allowing the diver to conserve their SCUBA air supply.

Weight belt: Not every diver uses a weight belt, but the majority do. The belts are designed to counteract the buoyancy of the diver and dive equipment. The weights are made from lead and are fitted to a webbed belt and have a quick release mechanism. Most divers require weights to achieve neutral or slightly negative buoyancy.

Now that we have covered SCUBA, lets have a look at the heavy gear:

Surface supplied air is generally considered deep-sea diving. Thus, some of the equipment is drastically different to SCUBA. Deep-sea diving is considered anything deeper than 60 feet, but normally operating between 150-300 feet.

Besides the depth, one of the main differences is the diving suit and helmet.

The **helmet** assembly was made from copper with bronze fittings. The view ports were heat treated sealed glass. A breast plate assembly connected the helmet to the diving suit, this was designed to distribute the weight of the helmet over the diver's shoulders affording the diver more comfort. The **diving suit** is constructed of vulcanized rubber, covering the entire body excluding the hands and head and creating a tough waterproof cover. When everything was connected the suit was airtight. I mentioned that the hands were excluded form the main suit, this was because the suit was sealed at the wrists by tight fitting rubber cuffs. Gloves were then fitted afterwards, typically in three finger design.

Weight belt: As SCUBA weights are needed, they even more so are required with deep-sea diving suit. Its approximate weight is 84 pounds. Each additional unit of lead weight was 7.5 pounds. So much weight is needed due to the positive buoyancy of the rubber suit.

Getting ready for a dive—checking SCUBA gear.

Diving shoes: These give protection and add additional weight to the divers feet. Adding the weight to the feet generally helps with the divers stability whilst underwater. The shoes were made of leather and canvas with hardwood inner sole, lead lower soles and capped with brass to protect the toes. They weighed around 35 pounds a pair.

Unlike SCUBA, the breathing material is supplied by a compressor from the surface, connected to the diver via an umbilical cord. Not only did this supply the diver with the mixture necessary to breath; it also slightly inflated the diving suit. The diver had the ability to adjust the air flowing into the helmet by using the "divers control valve" located on the helmet. Whilst in this heavy gear, the deep-sea diver is 100% reliant on the tenders, both in and out of the water.

The next stage of diving gear was just starting to be used when I was transitioning away from being a diver, so I never really had hands-on experience using one. These were called infinity or atmospheric suits. These giant suits of armor are rated for depths in excess of 2000 feet. They provide massive advantages over the old canvas deep-sea diver, no need for decompressing as it eliminates the need for mixed breathing materials. This allows for more bottom time, reducing the number of divers required.

The draw back to the infinity suit is the lack of dexterity and what they can't achieve now, in a few years they will. Infinity suits are the closest man will get to being a machine. Surely, we will be able to go deeper as technologies change and allow for better pressure resistance materials. But in the end, the diver is and has mostly already been replaced. Those ROV'S I mentioned prior, well, they are the future.

EPILOGUE

The day of the deep-sea diver is slowly dissolving into the unknown abyss. Gone are the days when women swooned if a man told her that he was a fearless, deep-sea diver.

Everyday, more and more machines take the place of the diver. ROV's are the future. They are able to work deeper, longer, and in worse conditions than the human body can cope with.

The diver will never truly be replaced, not 100%. Diving has become a way of life—a sport, recreational. The Scooby Doobys will always be around.

Looking back on my career as a Navy Frog Man and deep-sea diver. I was one of the lucky ones. I got to see marvelous things, fantastic creatures, and helped to shape the world we live in now. I worked hard and played hard. Along the way, I met some fantastic people whom I am proud to call friends.

If I had one regret in life . . . It was writing this damned book.

GLOSSARY

The following definitions of words and phrases have been prepared for your use. Assuming that if you are not already familiar with oil field terminology, nomenclature, slang, and general bullshit, you will be completely lost. So, consult this glossary often and you may learn something, and quite possibly, find a thing or two to chuckle about.

You may find that the words and phrases have a slightly different meaning than what you would expect to find in your copy of the unabridged Twentieth Century Dictionary. You will just have to trust me (sic) that the definitions I quote are the correct ones used in the offshore oil and diving industry. I make no apology if you find some of the words and terms offensive. There is no way that these words could be changed, without losing the flavor of their intent.

As that great British statesman and leader, Winston Churchill stated, "TWO GREAT NATIONS SEPARATED BY A COMMON LANGUAGE."

Never have truer words been spoken regarding the offshore oil industry and especially the diving industry in the North Sea.

ASS

A small, usually grey animal of the horse genus. A dull stupid fellow. Often used to denote the posterior of the female sex, also refers to her sexual capabilities, i.e., she's a great/lousy piece of ass.

ASSHOLE

The opening of the alimentary canal from which undigested residues are voided. A term of derision. An unpopular person, very often preceded by fucking, i.e., that fucking asshole.

BANG

An American term, meaning to have intercourse, i.e., give her a bang. The sound a letter bomb should make, that is unless it has been sent by a queer, in which case it will go POOF.

BASTARD

Self-explanatory

BELL

That which hangs in a church and goes ding dong. A saturation diver's favorite thing (next to, you know what) with a hole in its bottom.

BLOKE

A British term denoting, a guy, a fellow, maybe even an asshole.

BLOODY

A term the British apply to everything. A form of swearing, also a leaking of the body's fluids, i.e., a bloody nose, which an Englishman may receive if he were to call a Scotsman, a bloody Scot.

B.O.P.

An acronym, standing for, Blow Out Preventer.

BOSS

What a diver thinks he is. What a diver's wife most often is. Also see "wheel."

BOUNCE

A term used in diving to denote a quick dive, i.e., not saturation. Also, what large mammary glands on a female do very nicely.

BUBBLE HEAD

A deep-sea diver who may have had the dreaded bends just one time too many. Term most barge/ship captains use to refer to all divers.

BUG

A lobster. A Volkswagen car. A creepy crawler.

BUGGED

A state of agitation, what the Americans would call pissed off.

BUGGERY

Illicit love. Unlawful desires. Forbidden fruits.

BULL PRICK

The external organ of a bull. A term used in the diving industry to denote a tool used to align bolt holes underwater, you would call it a drift pin.

BULLSHIT

The undigested residue voided from a bull's alimentary canal. Unintelligible conversation from a bullshitter.

BULLSHITTER

A person known to have an unusual way with words. Very proficient speaker who speaks a lot of rubbish, otherwise known as bullshit.

CHICK

The young of fowls. A term of endearment to a young bird/girl, whom a diver spends a great deal of time chasing.

CHICKEN

A domestic fowl. Better known in the industry as a coward. When referring to the female of the species, this denotes an older bird as in 'FINGER LICKIN' GOOD.'

CHICKEN FEED

Small change, (except to a Scots). Importance, something of no importance, of no value.

CHICKEN SHIT

The undigested residue (let's forget this shit). A very unpopular person—a combination of an asshole, son of a bitch, and a bastard.

CHINK

A small hole in a wall. A person from Chinkyland.

CHINKY

A Chinese restaurant.

CHOW

A word denoting food. Mealtime. Sometimes refers to the ladies more delicious parts.

COCK

A male chicken. More likely to be referring to a diver's proudest possession.

COCK SUCKER

If male, a faggot. If female, a wonderful person that divers adore.

COME

A request or command from a very large, Norwegian waiter. (You thought it was going to be rude).

COME-A-LONG

A small hand operated winch similar to a chain fall. What a female says to a pussy whipped diver.

COON

A small rodent-like animal that COON-ASSES just love to hunt and eat. (Hah, got you again, you thought I was going to say it was a black person.)

COON-ASS

A person from Louisiana, a state in the southern part of the United States of America, from frog, (pardon me, I meant), French descent.

CRANK

An offset handle used to turn a winch or other types of mechanical devices. A diver's private parts that can be manipulated to get his motor running.

CRAP
Undigested residue voided from the alimentary canal, located on the face of a bullshitter.

CUNT
American slang to denote the private parts of the female gender, where the British equivalent would be FANNY. Also, an unkind reference to a fellow/bloke that is not likable.

D.D.C.
An acronym, standing for Deck Decompression Chamber (DDC).

DICK HEAD
See asshole for definition.

DIVER
An egotistical prima donna, who receives large sums of money to do, what other people pay to do. Sly, devious character always after someone's daughter. Normal habitat, large steel chambers, or a local pub (warning, association can be hazardous to your health).

DONKEY DICK
An adjustable stand off on a riser clamp, this assists in the alignment of the riser, origin of word unknown. It has been suggested that due to its appearance, similar to a donkey's erect sexual organ, the term may have originated from the similarity or appearance.

DONG
The sound a large church bell makes, i.e., dong, whereas a small church bell would make a ding, in other words DING-DONG.

ECHO

Sound that's heard when someone shouts between Slack Alice's thighs.

FAG

An English cigarette. An American queer.

FAGGOT

An Englishman smoking a cigarette.

FANNY

British slang expression for pussy, hair pie, fur burger, cunt, ass, etc., etc.

FILLED IN

British expression for getting your ass kicked.

FLICKING

Chinky mispronunciation of fucking.

FLOGGING

What the British did to their prisoners, and Aussies.

FLOGG'IN SPANNER

A wrench that you flog Aussies with. Or use underwater to tighten belts.

FROG

A little creature that has the capability to jump long distances. A French delicacy. Things the British people don't like.

FUCK

A word frequently used in the oil patch. (If you removed this word from a diver's vocabulary, his conversations would be 50% shorter.)

FUCKED

A word used to indicate that a piece of equipment is no longer functional. Or a very drunk diver.

FUCKING

A prefix to diver.

FUCK YOU

A term of endearment that a drunk diver would say to that giant Norwegian waiter (see come for enlightenment). If the diver uses this statement in this situation, he may very well end up fucked as well.

FUR BURGER

An American delicacy, usually associated with the female gender of the species.

GASED

A state of intoxication. When someone hyperphalates in a crowded room.

HAIR PIE

A diver's favorite midnight snack that can only be gotten at the "Y".

HAND

What almost all divers have two of. What a diver expects after a good performance of Gorilla Theater. A hand is a term used to denote that a crewmember is a good member of that team.

HEAVY GEAR
What a diver wears when he has a heavy date, or the old fashion diving suits seen in the movies.

HERO
A guy that rides a big white horse.

HORSE
What a HERO rides.

HUNG
What a horse is, and what all divers would like to be.

HYPERPHALATE
Foul smelling gas passed from the alimentary canal of a diver, more commonly known as a fart.

INDIAN
The poor asshole that does all the work because everybody else is a chief.

JOCK
Slang term for a Scotsman. A configuration of elastic and straps designed to hold up an athlete's smelly testicles.

JULIET
The tenth letter in the phonetic alphabet. Also, a faggot in Antwerp.

KILO
The eleventh letter in the phonetic alphabet, and how a Mexican pronounces, kill all yankee bastards, i.e., kilo yankee bastards.

KNOB

What is hanging on the end of a well-hung horse, and what the majority of divers think they have.

KNOBBY

British slang for shark.

LIMEY

An English Gentleman. (sic).

MUFF

A prefix to diver, i.e., muff diver, also, a warm furry thing with a hole in the middle, handy to put your fingers into to keep them warm.

NUT

Divers are often referred to as nuts. Also handy for putting into a jock strap.

ON THE JOB

British slang meaning to have sexual intercourse. American meaning, to work.

PISS

Excretory product, usually amber liquid, of the kidneys, chief means of voiding nitrogenous waste. More frequently used to denote a poor quality of beer.

PISSED

British slang to signify a state of intoxication. American meaning, nitrogenous waste had been voided.

PISSED OFF

American slang, meaning to be irate, angry, etc.

PISSED ON

This term denotes that you just been had, same meaning as shit on. Check your back for stab wounds.

PISS ARTIST

Individual who is very accomplished in the art of consuming large quantities of strong alcoholic drink. Also proficient at painting the town.

PLICK

A mispronunciation of the word prick by a Chinky. see flicking. e.g., "you flicking plick".

PLONK

What the British call BOOZE.

PRICK

A diver's pride and joy, and some of the ladies as well. Also, can be used to indicate that a fellow is not a nice guy, i.e., "You fucking prick." Please note, the Chinese would pronounce this term as flicking plick.

PUKE

The undigested residue voided from the other end of the alimentary canal of a sick diver who has over indulged while on the piss. (That sounds like a lot of shit to me.)

PUSSY
If you haven't figured out what pussy is by now, there is no hope for you, so, just fuck off. Also, if you call a man a pussy, you are telling him you think he is a wimp.

QUEER
My Funk and Wagnall says, odd, singular, quaint, open to suspicion, slightly mad, sick, ill. (Have you ever heard so much bullshit in your whole life?)

RADAR
What divers have as a natural sense, for locating hot pussy.

RANCH
What a Texan calls a wrench.

RANK
The smell of a diver's fart. An officer and a gentleman's rate.

R.O.V.
An acronym, standing for Remote Operated Vehicle (ROV).

SATURATION
What a pissed diver is. A diving term denoting that a diver's tissue are completely full of inert gases.

SCOTSMAN
A means of spending your money while he saves his.

SCUBA
An acronym meaning, self-contained underwater breathing apparatus. A piece of diving gear a 'scubby dooby' would find helpful to commit unintentional suicide.

S.D.C.
An acronym meaning, Submersible Decompressed Chamber (SDC).

SHIT/SHITE
The undigested residue voided from the alimentary canal (seems like we heard this shit somewhere before). Excrement. A contemptuous term for a person. To evacuate the bowels. Expressing annoyance, disappointment. All of the above is right straight out of my old Funk and Wagnall.

SON-OF-A-BITCH
No definition required.

SURFACE
The place a submerged diver wishes he was.

STANDARD GEAR
The gear a diver would wear for an ordinary date, see heavy gear.

STROKE
What the Chief Cook has, what a diver wishes be had, what a woman wants.

STUFF
Whatever diver likes to do to young sweet things.

TELLY
An English word slang for Television

T.L.P.
An acronym standing for, Transfer Lock Personnel (TLP).

T.U.P.
An acronym standing for, Transfer Under Pressure (TUP).

UP
A direction a diver must never forget. But most often used with an upward gesture of two upright fingers, while saying "up yours."

VOLUME
A scale of measurement, usually in pint mugs, used to determine how much beer you can drink.

WATER
A fluid, which in microscopic quantities you add to whisky.

WANKER
Wanker used the same as jack-off, the verb being, wanking. Englishmen's favorite pass time.

WHEEL
A common term to denote the man in charge, i.e. the boss, a wheel. Also, what a dog pisses on.

WOP
The sound a kilo of shit makes when thrown against a wall.

WOPMOBILE

Any one of the several makes of hand-built, Italian sports cars.

X-RAY

What fries your chromosomes on a long pipeline job.

X-RATED

An applicable handle for all divers. A diver's thought when he sees a good-looking bird.

YANK

A considerate term of endearment that the British use to denote an American. What an American does to his PUD.

ZEED

Decompression table designation to indicate that you are all burned out, washed up, finished.

ZEES

What you find in comic books to denote sleep i.e., zzzzzzzzzzzzzz's. What this book most likely did to you.

www.ingramcontent.com/pod-product-compliance
Lightning Source LLC
Chambersburg PA
CBHW070349090426
42733CB00009B/1344